WIN OR LOSE?

WIN OR LOSE?

What You Should Know
About the ERA

Collis H. White

EXPOSITION PRESS   **HICKSVILLE, NEW YORK**

Grateful acknowledgment is made to the Associated Press and to *U.S. News and World Report* for permission to reprint excerpts from their articles.

Copyright 1975 *U.S. News & World Report*, Inc.

Reprinted by permission of the Associated Press, New York.

FIRST EDITION

ISBN 0-682-48596-9

Printed in the United States of America

40774

To my lovely wife Gladys

Contents

Contents

Preface

This book is written for the purpose of sharing with the reader the philosophy and actions of the Women's Liberation Movement, the effects of such philosophy and actions on woman, on man, on child, and on society, together with the predicted effects of the Equal Rights Amendment, should it become law.

My experience in these matters has been enriched by my students in classes of sociology and constitutional law in the colleges in which I have recently taught, added to my experience in the practice of law.

To me, the ultimate happiness in life is found with freedom in relations between husband and wife, between parent and child, between man and woman of whatever status, in relations among members of families, in one's freedom to believe, to act, and to grow without hostile and frustrating experiences brought about by unreasonable restraints imposed by others or imposed by governments.

I believe in a happy and successful marriage, in a stable and happy relationship between parent and child, in a happy and workable relationship between employer and employee, in the right to privacy, in the right to freedom, both in religious beliefs and religious practice, all free of unreasonable control by government or control by others.

It appears to me that the philosophy and actions of the Women's Liberation Movement will destroy such happy and workable relations because such philosophy and actions will result in war by woman against man and in war by man against woman, with children being used as tools in the process of such wars. In fact, the Women's Liberation Movement has already caused some bitter and hostile relations between man and woman

9

with its anti-male philosophy and with demands that women be allowed to compete with men in all areas of life.

Should the Equal Rights Amendment become law, the amendment will be used as a tool by the leaders of the Women's Liberation Movement to hopefully force a "balance of sexual integration" in all social and economic and political life, irrespective of needs, qualifications, and desires.

The real aim of the Women's Liberation Movement is to use the Equal Rights Amendment as a tool, in my opinion, for the sole purpose of bringing about a new structure in relations between man and woman, between parent and child, between employer and employee, in sex life, in marriage, in family relations, and in all social and economic and political life, all suitable to the specifications and philosophy of the leaders of the Movement.

Thus the arguments of the supporters and proponents for the Equal Rights Amendment are deceptive and misleading, since the Equal Rights Amendment will have little if anything to do with legitimate legal rights, but be concerned solely with the psychological and philosophical conflicts advanced by the motivates of the leaders of the Movement.

Passage of the Equal Rights Amendment can result only in losses for woman, for man, for child, and for society.

WIN OR LOSE?

1

Demand for Change

The aim of the Women's Liberation Movement is to change the entire structure in human relations.

As a tool for accomplishing this aim the Movement hopes to have the proposed Equal Rights Amendment ratified and adopted as the Twenty-seventh Amendment to the United States Constitution.

The demands for changes by the Women's Liberation Movement are radically revolutionary. They are intended to affect the entire thread which holds society together. This we shall see while going through our discussions.

We want to determine the predicted gains and losses for man, woman, child, and society, should the amendment become law.

In our discussions, at times, we'll use the term *Movement* for the term *Women's Liberation Movement* and use the term *ERA* for the term *Equal Rights Amendment*.

Let's keep in mind that the proposed ERA grew out of the Movement's clamor for changes in human relations, and that the ERA is intended to further the philosophy and actions of the Movement. After analyzing the expected use to be made of the ERA by the Movement, we'll see that the ERA will in no way bring about and promote equality of rights for women, or for anyone else for that matter.

To the contrary, we'll see that the ERA will, if it becomes law, bring about and usher in a field of inequality of rights. Also we'll see that the ERA will in no way serve any legitimate purpose for anyone. The consequences of such a law would be chaotic.

The Movement's demands for changes adversely go to the very heart of relations between husband and wife, relations between parent and child, relations in sex, relations involving the concept of marriage, relations involving legal divorce, relations involving the growth and development of children, relations involving the family as an institution, relations between man and woman in matters of church and religion, relations between man and woman in businesses and professions, and relations between male and female in schools and colleges and universities.

Of course the demands of the Movement have already had many social and legal implications. No-fault divorce is, to some extent, in my opinion, the result of demands for more rights by women. Alimony for men is another social and legal implication. The wife's contribution to child support after legal divorce is another.

The increase in our divorce rate is also one. As women have increasingly demanded that they be treated or accepted on the same level with men, our courts have, in the social and legal processes, recognized some of the demands. In doing so, the courts have placed more responsibility on women. In my opinion, the trend is that, as the social and legal processes recognize new and additional demands from women, the processes will also impose additional duties on women.

Yet, in disregard of setbacks for women as a result of the philosophy and actions by the Movement, the war against society by the Movement rages on and on and on!

The irate cry for equal rights for women has been ringing from the lips of a few militant women in the halls of Congress, in the corridors of state legislatures, and in the news media, all across our land. The few militant women have been the promoters, organizers, and directors for lobbying activities in support of the ERA. They come from the Movement. We find them in such groups as the National Organization for Women, the National Federation of Business and Professional Women's Club, Inc., Common Cause, the National Women's Political Caucus, and the League of Women Voters.

The few militant women denounce and renounce men, marriage, and children to some extent, all as means of control over women. They boldly announce that woes and troubles of woman have been fostered and imposed on woman by man.

Then there's the less militant group of women who constitute a sizable number and who have not gone so far as to denounce and renounce marriage, husbands, and children. This group of women waver on the thought of not so hot for equal rights for women but, "If it means more rights for women, let us have them!" They're not just sure what "it" means. This group tends to be followers of the militant few. Yet, the group believes in a happy husband-wife and parent-child relationship.

The third group of women who are followers of the militant few fall into the "me-too" category. The militant woman shouts, "I want equal rights with men! I want to be a first-class citizen!" The members of the me-too group resound with, "me, too!" Its members jump on the bandwagon which sings with a loud halleujah of the Promised Land for women.

They are obedient but ill-advised followers of the militant few. They do as told by both the militant and the not-so-militant groups. Like their leaders, they can write letters to their state legislator, vote, and seek votes in the name of the Promised Land for Women, which carries the American-sounding virtue of Equal Rights, more specifically equal rights for women!

The next group of women which constitutes a great majority of American women is opposed, with some feeling neutral, to the ERA. This group sees and feels a threat by both the Movement and the proposed ERA to the special and protected position of the woman in our society. They feel and see the need of a happy husband-wife and parent-child relationship. They cherish the feminine virtues of woman and feel proud and take pride in being a woman. Unlike the other groups, this group seems to have members who are fairly well adjusted to man and woman both living in, and enjoying, the same society.

While the militant few, the not-so-militant group, and the me-toos have been well organized and have had forceful and vocal leadership, the great majority of women who in effect oppose the Movement and the ERA have had little organization and little leadership and, therefore, no effective opposition to the views espoused by the Movement in respect to the ERA. However, this great majority started gaining momentum in the year 1974 and made itself heard in the state legislatures, as we shall shortly see by the actions taken by the legislatures for the years 1974 and 1975.

Then there's the next group: men. They have sat in ringside seats, watching the Movement and the hopes of the proponents of the ERA with relish and amazement, with laughter and excitement, with disgust and confusion, with apathy, and, in general, with little heed to the poisonous medicine about to be injected into man-woman, husband-wife, and parent-child relationships, should the ERA become law.

So the Movement has gone on with momentum, little restrained in respect to the ratification of the ERA, until the year 1974. Unruly emotions have been the winner over common sense. Demands by the Movement have prevailed over the needs of women and over deliberate and sound judgment of considered consequences of the demands.

Being preoccupied with other matters, being little informed of the consequences of the ERA, and being tired of the agitators of the Movement for support of the ERA, our Congress passed the proposed Equal Rights Acts in March of 1972. If adopted by thirty-eight of the state legislatures, by March, 1979, the act will become the twenty-seventh amendment to the U.S. Constitution. On the other hand, if the act is not ratified by this number of the state legislatures, by March of 1979, the act will die.

In the beginning, the act was ratified by state legislatures, with a bang! However, ratification is now, as of September, 1975, at a standstill. Fourteen state legislatures considered the ERA for ratification in the year 1975, as of August 29, but only one ratified it; only three states ratified it in the year 1974, while eight states ratified it in the year 1973. But, in the year 1972, the year in which Congress passed the act, twenty-two states ratified the act. You can see that, beginning with the year 1974, the state legislatures began to have second thoughts about the wisdom of ratifying the act.

According to information compiled by the Library of Congress, as of August 29, 1975, thirty-four state legislatures have ratified the ERA, with two of these states rescinding ratification, which is subject to doubtful legality in respect to the validity of recission by the two states.

The thirty-four states which have ratified the ERA as of August 29, 1975, with two recissions, and dates of ratification are as follows:

2/03/75—North Dakota
2/07/74—Ohio
1/21/74—Montana
1/18/74—Maine
3/22/73—Washington
3/15/73—Connecticut
2/21/73—Vermont
2/12/73—New Mexico
2/08/73—Minnesota
2/08/73—Oregon
2/02/73—South Dakota
1/24/73—Wyoming
11/13/72—California
9/20/72—Pennsylvania
6/21/72—Massachusetts
6/15/72—Kentucky
5/26/72—Maryland
5/22/72—Michigan
5/03/72—New York
4/22/72—West Virginia
4/21/72—Colorado
4/20/72—Wisconsin
4/17/72—New Jersey
4/14/72—Rhode Island
4/05/72—Alaska
4/04/72—Tennessee (voted to rescind 4/23/74)
3/30/72—Texas
3/28/72—Kansas
3/24/72—Idaho

3/24/72—Iowa
3/23/72—Delaware
3/23/72—Nebraska (voted to rescind 3/15/73)
3/23/72—New Hampshire
3/22/72—Hawaii

Assuming that the two recissions are valid, we have thirty-two states which have ratified the ERA, leaving a need for six more states to ratify. However, if the two recissions are not constitutional, then we need only four more ratifications. There is no legal precedent for determining whether or not a state can constitutionally rescind its ratification of a proposal to the U.S. Constitution.

The proponents of the ERA may be in for trouble, because the people and the state legislatures are becoming more educated about the effects of the ERA, should it become law. There is presently, at the time of this writing, negative feeling about the wisdom of making the ERA a law. These feelings seem to prevail over the positive feelings in support of the ERA as law. Only time will tell.

There are sixteen states which have not ratified the ERA, not counting the two states which have voted to rescind ratification. The sixteen are Alabama, Arizona, Arkansas, Florida, Georgia, Illinois, Indiana, Louisiana, Mississippi, Missouri, Nevada, North Carolina, Oklahoma, South Carolina, Utah, and Virginia. Of these sixteen states, thirteen of them definitely considered ratification in the 1975 sessions of the state legislatures, as of August 29, but failed to ratify the ERA. The remaining three states are Alabama, Mississippi, and Arkansas. The chance of the ERA being ratified by these three states is rather slim, because they are conservative and will take a conservative position on a proposal which is as radical as the proposed ERA.

Yet, the wind to opposition may change its course. One never knows just how or when the social and political climate may change in the American society. The Movement is regrouping, as we shall see in the next chapter, with the objectives of more members in its fold, better organization, and more money. The

Movement plans a big and bloody campaign in the year 1976 for the purpose of persuading the remaining state legislatures to give the needed votes to the ratification of the ERA.

The language of the ERA reads as follows:

> Equality of rights under the law shall not be denied or abridged by the United States or by any State on the account of sex.

Fair enough! Fair enough, that is, when looking solely to the language of the proposed amendment. However, what does the language mean? What rights are included or excluded? What duties are included? Are the rights and duties definable or identifiable? Do the rights and duties extend to both government and private actions? Will the ERA take away the right to privacy in homes, in the family, and in religion, as well as in other areas of private life? As we wade through our discussions, we'll attempt to answer these questions.

Do the rights include every possible complaint which could possibly arise because of alleged sex discrimination, depending just who wants to sue whom for what? Very likely, there is not a single area of living in our society, which includes marriage, divorce, alimony, child support, care and visitation rights to children, crimes, business, professions, labor, churches, schools, and all other areas of American life that cannot be labelled in a lawsuit as sex discrimination, should the ERA become law.

What courts will enforce the amendment if it becomes law? The federal courts, of course. The judges of these courts are not trained to hear and decide local disputes in family matters, nor in other domestic matters at community levels. Think of what the federal courts have done and are still doing in racial discrimination cases involving alleged discrimination in school situations, taking away the needs and desires of the people by forced busing and by other means. The ERA will spread to and control private life much more so than has been the case in civil rights matters, should the ERA become law.

In considering the proposed ERA, we should consider that

we already have sufficient laws to do away with all unfair sex discrimination, as we shall see in chapter 4. We don't need laws which will perpetuate fighting and bickering over unfounded and illegitimate claims between man and woman, between husband and wife, and between parent and child. The proposed ERA will, however, bring about just such laws should it be ratified and become a part of the U.S. Constitution.

The Movement hopes to force man and woman to live by its proposed standards when the ERA becomes law, if it does. Under the ERA all distinctions of rights and duties between man and woman are to be abolished, not voluntarily but by law if need be. There are to be no more distinctions in any respect between man and woman under the ERA. This is the primary goal of the Movement in its quest for the ERA as law.

The ERA is not only an enemy to democracy but a proposed law which in no way will work in our society. If the proposed ERA is to be nondiscriminatory, it can't favor man in one instance, simply because he is a man, nor favor woman in another, simply because she is a woman. The ERA will not allow for flexibility, which is always needed in the law in order to meet the flexible needs of the people.

Under the proposed ERA, if a man is to be legally subjected to military draft, so should a woman; if a fit mother is entitled to custody of minor children, so is a fit father; if a woman is entitled to use a particular public bathroom, so is a man; if a man can go topless on the beach or go topless in a bar or lounge, so can a woman; if a husband can legally be charged for his wife's necessaries, so can a wife be legally charged for her husband's necessaries.

There is no end to the road in doing away with distinctions between man and woman, should the ERA become law. Without the existence for flexibility in distinctions between man and woman, life will become rather chaotic and meaningless, in all economic and social and political respects.

A woman can't choose to use the ERA as law when convenient to her and ignore it at all other times. The same applies to a man. The difference between man and woman in this regard is that many women are laboring under the false assumption that they can use the law to enable them to play two roles: one of special and protected femininity and one of having all rights accorded to them without the duties which accompany those rights. Not so! If the law is to be fair and nondiscriminatory to both man and woman, its duties must be equally imposed on both.

Nor should a woman be entitled to a job or to any other position in life simply because she is a woman, should the ERA become law. For example, a woman shouldn't be entitled to walk into an employer's office and say, "I can do the job, and, because I'm a woman, give the job to me." Being a woman will not automatically make her entitled to a job which can be filled by a man who has qualifications equal to or superior to her qualifications.

This is true, even though women are now given preferential treatment in respect to jobs and other positions, at the expense of discriminating against men, as we shall see in chapter 4. Of course the Movement hopes to give the woman even more preferential treatment under the ERA, if it becomes law. In other words, the Movement seeks not equality of rights for women but more rights for women and fewer for men. This is the one major aim of the Movement's hope under the ERA. Put another way, the Movement hopes to take away rights for some and give them to others, irrespective of needs and qualifications.

Far too many women will be disillusioned by the supposed advantages and benefits to be had from the ERA. The disadvantages imposed by the ERA will far outweigh the advantages that women have traditionally enjoyed.

The ERA will lower the status of women if it becomes law, as will the philosophy and actions of the Movement. We'll be discussing these points in detail later on.

At this point, let me warn you that many persons will accuse you and me, or anyone else, of being unamerican if we say that we're against the proposed ERA. They'll say, "How can you be against the ERA if you believe that this great nation of ours was founded and has thrived on equality?" The term "equal rights" is part of our deep-bedded American heritage. In American life, a person can't be American and at the same time be openly against equal rights. This is one of the arguments which the Movement has used in support of ratification of the ERA.

Keep this in mind: the term "equal rights" as used in connection with the ERA is deceptive and misleading. Equal rights don't mean equal rights when considered in connection with the proposed ERA. We'll talk more about this in chapter 3.

On Friday, March 14, 1975, I was in Milton, Florida, talking to a very fine member of the Florida Legislature, Ed Fortune, about the upcoming legislative session which was to convene in April of 1975. One of the issues for consideration was to be ratification of the ERA. Ratification was defeated in the 1974 session. Ed said that he voted for ratification of the ERA in the 1974 session because he ". . . felt that everyone should be for equal rights . . ." which view is the main thrust of the Movement for support of the ERA.

However, he stated that he would vote against the ERA in the 1975 session because what he understood to be equal rights in the ERA would not be equal rights! Ratification would, in his opinion, result in damage to women and not at all equal rights for them.

By pressure and misleading use of the label "equal rights," the Movement has, in the beginning, mustered great support for the ERA. However, after time and study of the nature and consequences of the proposed ERA, many persons, including legislators, are convinced that the ERA would not be good for women or for anyone else.

The ERA will, used along with the philosophy and actions of the Movement, result in loss of identity for woman; result in taking away her historical dignity as a woman, as well as taking away her image of femininity; result in causing her to have to lose custody of minor children in divorce cases, lose child support, and to fend for herself; result in loss of protection which has been reserved for her by history.

However, if she is to be on the same footing as man in all

respects, as advocated by the Movement, she'll be treated as a man in all respects.

Also the ERA will, used along with the philosophy and actions of the Movement, result in hostile and frustrated relations between husband and wife, between man and woman in all classes, between parent and child; result in the abolishment of the family as an institution in many cases.

The ERA will, used along with the philosophy and actions of the Movement, result in an increase in homosexuality; result in an increase in the divorce rate; result in brainwashing boy and girl against each other, against marriage, against children, against family, and against life itself, to a large extent.

Too, the ERA will result in government bureaucrats and federal courts taking away privacy and personal freedom of the American citizen.

Since the ERA is a tool to be used by the Movement in attaining its goals, we must first understand and appreciate the philosophy and actions of the Movement, if we are to understand and appreciate the predicted effects of the ERA.

2

Philosophy and Actions of the Movement

The philosophy of the Movement is a form of radicalism which has intended actions for the purpose of bringing about revoluntary changes in human relations involving marriage, divorce, parent and child, the family, sexual relations, religion, morality, and also changes in the general areas of the social, the economic, and the political worlds.

The ultimate aim of the Movement is to change the entire structure of human relations, and the approach to be used in achieving this aim is to completely eradicate all differences in identities and attitudes which make distinctions between man and woman.

The end result is to be a bar against references to sex in any form of classification which would make any distinction between a woman and man.

Therefore, in order to achieve this ultimate aim, the Movement feels that the proposed ERA, as a law, is necessary in order to codify and enforce the philosophy and actions of the Movement. We'll get to the predicted legal meaning of the proposed ERA in detail in the next chapter.

Before discussing specific areas of philosophy and actions, let's take a brief look at the form and structure of the Movement.

The cry for women's rights is not new. For example, we had the women's suffrage amendment—the nineteenth—ratified and adopted as a part of the U.S. Constitution in 1920. Also, many years ago, all state legislatures abolished the common-law doctrine, which denied the rights of a married woman to contract in her name, own property, convey property, and gave to her many other rights which were denied at common law.

There is a clear difference, however, between woman's quest for rights which existed heretofore and the quest for rights by the present Movement. The demands for rights which existed prior to the present Movement had specific objectives which could clearly be pointed out with reason, but the demands by the present Movement have no specific and meaningful objectives, including the proposed ERA, and the demands seem to flow from deep and unrecognizable frustration, as we shall see throughout this book.

The present Movement was hardly recognized by the general public until after the year of 1963, when Betty Friedan's book, *The Feminine Mystique* was published. Since then, there has been a wave of discontentment among some women, primarily the staunch supporters of both the Movement and the ERA.

In the 1960s, commissions in all fifty states were formed in order to study the status of women. This period also gave birth to organizations in support of rights for women. Now carrying the banner for women are such organizations as the National Organization for Women (NOW), The National Federation of Business and Professional Women's Club, Inc., Common Cause, the National Women's Political Caucus, and the League of Women Voters.

The Movement has increased to several million supporters, keeping in mind that not every supporter will be an official member of an organization, and that some men are supporters of the Movement.

There's a drive to increase support for the Movement and its aims. For example, some twenty-three million women plan a fund-raising drive for the ratification of the ERA by the nation's birthday in the year of 1976, as reported by the Associated Press.[1] Also, the Commission to Commemorate International Women's Year has made the ERA its top priority.

Members of the various women's organizations include women

---

[1]The *Mobile Register,* May 20, 1975, p. 5-A.

from many segments of life. However, based on my observations, the leaders and chief supporters of the Movement are the single woman, the divorced woman, and the unhappily married woman, although I have no statistics as to actual members for any particular category of women in respect to membership in the organizations.

As its modus operandi (method of operation) the Movement has, to a rather large extent, duplicated the activism of the Civil Rights Movement and the Student Revolutionary Movement of the 1960s. You'll recall that these movements were well organized at all levels in the various communities, with demands for actions, sometimes resulting in sit ins, demonstrations, violence, and other tactics, as well as with legal actions. Be that as it may, the two movements did receive attention to their cause, whether justified or not.

Like these two Movements, the present Women's Movement is organized from a grass-roots level, from city, to county, to state, to national, and to international levels. All levels have been fairly well unified in purpose and tactics, as were the Civil Rights Movement and the Student Revolutionary Movement.

As the Civil Rights Movement has said, and still says, that its members have been oppressed, suppressed, and made subservient by and for the convenience of the white man, the present Women's Movement has said, and still says, that women have been oppressed, suppressed, and made subservient by man and for the pleasures of man.

In the next chapter we'll see striking similarities in methods and procedures and objectives, as well as striking similarities in the philosophy, between the Civil Rights Movement and the Women's Liberation Movement.

The Women's Movement has no specific objectives in its quest to do away with the present structure of relations between man and woman, as well as relations in other areas in which women are associated; nor does the Movement have any specific and logical objectives in its aim to have the ERA ratified and adopted as law. We can, however, look at some of the aims, which, if

adopted, would definitely do away with the present requirements
in such areas as marriage, divorce, relations between parent and
child, and relations in other areas of the religious, moral, social,
economic, and political worlds.

Perhaps the general philosophy and actions of the Movement
can be generally summed up by what was reported, by the
Associated Press, to have been said by Imelda Marcos, wife of
President Ferdinand E. Marcos of the Philippines, while speaking
at the International Women's Year Conference in Mexico City,
Mexico, in June of 1975, which is as follows:

> . . . the feminist movement in the United States and other
> prosperous nations has become too competitive, demanding
> and anti-male.
>
> The demand for equality has too often had overtones of
> revenge, the venting of grievances, the acquisition of advan-
> tage, the aggression of concealed hatred and envy. . . .[2]

Let's analyze what she has said.

It boils down to this: The Movement demands that a woman
be allowed to compete with man in every phase of life, regardless
of needs, aptitudes, physical ability, and practicality for her to do
so. Neither does the Movement consider man's needs and wishes
in the respect to competition.

In many cases, which we'll shortly discuss in this chapter and
in succeeding chapters, the attempts to compete with man have
no rational or justifiable basis. The attempts are the Movement's
aggressive aims which will result only in venting woman's frustration with man, blaming man for woman's unhappiness, when
causes for her unhappiness lie in herself, caused by her inability
to adjust happily to life with man.

The attempts are ways to get at man—blame him! Her blame
placed on man is her way of attacking man for her maladjustment to life. She sees him as being responsible for her lot in
life, and the way to justify one's shortcomings is to shift the

---

[2]The *Mobile Register,* June 21, 1975, p. 2-A.

blame to another. So, the Movement seeks to vehemently transfer woman's supposed shortcomings to man.

Such a woman's feelings or thoughts are, "I'll show him! I'll teach him! I'll let him know that I'm as good as he is and equal to him." Then she says, "I'll use *Ms.* instead of *Mrs.* and make him use it, and I'll use my maiden name instead of his name when we're married." So, she seeks to do everything possible to wipe out any distinctions which may exist between her and man, but yet she attempts to retain some form of separate identity, such as using her maiden name instead of her husband's name, as a lesson for him to know that she is his equal.

So it goes, woman seeking to reject identity with man while seeking recognition from him. True, every person needs individuality, but this is not the case with the Movement. The Movement doesn't see that individuality and mutual existence between a man and woman must and can only exist by allowing man to be himself and by allowing woman to be herself, while, at the same time happily coexisting.

The Movement hopes to abolish all present structures in relations between man and woman and, after this is done, establish identities for a woman and for a man, suitable to the philosophy of the Movement, whatever it may be.

Yet, the very things which the Movement seeks are identity for woman and recognition of this identity by man. But such is sought from an anti-male approach and anti-male philosophy.

Until the Movement rids itself of such anti-male philosophy and actions, goals for equality with man (which are primarily mental in nature without actually existing), will never be realized, because such philosophy and actions will bring to woman only resentment and rejection and retaliation from man. A feeling of equality can't be realized without mutual and willing cooperation between man and woman.

But the Movement doesn't believe in a spirit of mutual cooperation based on needs and desires between man and woman. It has given immediate mandates to man for changes in relations between man and woman, or else! The Movement is unaware of, or else ignores, that a free and voluntary relationship between a man and woman is the only kind of relationship which is desirable and productive.

For example, the Movement demands that all fields of employment be equally open to woman and man, that all distinctions based on sex in fitness for employment be eradicated. Yet, we know that such demands are unrealistic and impracticable. A woman and a man each have differences in aptitudes, differences in physical abilities, and differences in goals in life which make some jobs or positions suitable more to one sex than to the other.

It is generally assumed that a woman has an aptitude for greater ability in positions that require detailed work and better aptitude in some areas of the arts and sciences than man. On the other hand, it is generally assumed that man has a greater aptitude in jobs or positions that may be involved with violence than does woman. For instance, generally it can be assumed that a man would be more emotionally stable than a woman on the front lines of a battlefield in time of war. Also some women don't have the physical ability to perform certain jobs which are commonly handled by man.

Along with differences between a man and woman in the areas of aptitudes and physical ability is the issue of ambition or interest in goals in life. Many times, one's goal is geared to his or her aptitude as well as to physical ability and to ambition.

So, why is it unfair or a denial of rights to women if jobs or positions are classified according to sex in some areas of employment? It is submitted that some jobs or positions can't be performed except by classification based on sex. The Movement's mandates to do away with such classification is nowhere near realistic or practical or desirable.

Along with demands for eradication of all distinctions between man and woman in the economic areas is the Movement's demands for total eradication of distinctions between them in the area of politics. The Movement states that, using the modus operandi (method of operation), and philosophy of the Civil Rights Movement, more women should be appointed to judgeships and to other positions in politics. The Women's Movement demands that a certain percentage of all positions be filled by women, regardless of needs and qualifications.

In other words, as the Civil Rights Movement has demanded and has received and hopes for more positions based purely on race, the women's Movement has demanded and has received and hopes for more positions based purely on sex. As the Civil Rights Movement has said, "Give the position to me, because I'm Black or Chinese," or whatever, the Women's Movement has said, "Give the position to me because I'm a woman."

As the Civil Rights Movement has used discrimination based on race in order to discriminate against the majority, the Women's Movement is using, and hopes to use, discrimination based on sex in order to discriminate against man. The philosophy and actions of both Movements have striking similarities. The Women's Movement has reasoned that the Civil Rights Movement has been successful, so why not adopt the philosophy and actions of the Civil Rights Movement.

Yet, I ask, "How in good faith can the Women's Movement urge the ratification and adoption of the ERA as a law which is intended to do away with all discrimination based on sex, when, in fact, it is the very aim of the Movement to use the ERA in order to justify discrimination based on sex?"

The American people don't need such a deceptive law.

Economics and politics are not the only areas in which the Movement seeks complete eradication of distinctions between man and woman. The same aim is sought in religion. Witness the eleven women who, at the time of this writing, had been admitted to priesthood by a priest in the Episcopal Church, resulting in a court trial in Akron, Ohio in order to determine the women's demands and the priest's action in admitting them into priesthood.

So, the Movement also seeks to have its demands take precedence before the ordinances and religious convictions of certain religious orders are satisfied. If the Movement has its way, churches will have to establish new structures, allowing women in any position, in churches which have, heretofore, been available only to men.

While the demands for competition by the Movement in the areas in which we've been discussing are new changes in relations for man and woman, by far the areas which will be affected in drastic ways by the philosophy and actions of the Movement, if allowed its way, are those dealing with marriage, divorce, relations between husband and wife, relations between parent and child, as well as the standards of morality to be applied to these relations. In addition, the legal responsibility to be applied in these areas is a matter of concern to the members who will be affected, should the Movement have its way.

At least some supporters of the Movement hope to accomplish a relationship for a man and a woman which would allow them to live together without the formality of being married, have children without being legally married, if they so desire, all free of any social stigma which has been and presently is attached to such relations.

Along with these changes is the suggestion that men, women, and children live together in communes, if they so desire, with any and all being responsible for the welfare of each other, with no legal responsibility being pinned on any one person.

Within the demands for changes in the area of man-and-woman relations, are sexual relations which include a demand that a woman be allowed an abortion if she becomes pregnant, without being restrained by laws and also without social stigma being attached to an abortion. The Movement believes that a woman should have sole discretion as to an abortion, without consent from the husband, the lover, or from anyone else.

In cases where there is a marriage, a mother is not to be any more responsible for staying home and caring for the young children of the marriage than is the father. Both should be allowed the equal right to work outside the home in pursuing a career.

In support of such philosophy and actions, let's take a look at some of the views of Gloria Steinem, an editor of *Ms.* magazine, as reported in an interview reprinted from *U. S. News and World Report* in an article entitled "Women's Lives Will Change in Every Way," a portion of which follows:

Q: How will families be affected?

A: Already, there is a variety of alternatives available, and that's the real point of the change. It's not that we want to replace the old imperative of the patriarchal nuclear family—father, mother and children—with a new imperative, because any single system would be wrong for many people. There must be a variety of options—so that it becomes an honorable solution to remain single, to live with another person, to have children or not to have children, and so on.

Q: Will children gain or lose by this process?

A: I don't see how they could lose. First of all, they would be wanted, not just thought of as something "everybody does." And right now, in addition to being tracked along masculine or feminine lines, kids rarely have any community of their own until they get to school.

In the future, there will be more communal situations in which children will be around a variety of adults, as well as other nonrelated "family" members who are children of various ages. . . .

At present there's no real understanding that kids also need their own peers in addition to adults in their lives, before they get to school and in their living situations. We badly need more communal situations and less isolation and ghettoization of people according to age or class or sex. . . .

Q: How will the lives of women change?

A: In every way. Autonomy—the ability to control our own bodies and work identities and futures—is a revolution for women. . . .

Responsibility for children won't be exclusively the woman's any more, but shared equally by men—and shared by the community, too. That means that work patterns will change for both women and men, and women can enter all fields just as men can.

It used to be said that women couldn't succeed in work because they didn't have wives. In the future, men won't have "wives" either—not in the traditional, subservient sense.[3]

Should the recommendations of Ms. Steinem be accepted by society they would create a world of problems for man and woman and child.

What would be problems for a man and woman living together without being legally married? In many cases they will desert each other when the first major quarrel between them occurs. When the chips are down, it's likely that most couples who are living together without being legally married will not feel and acknowledge obligations to each other in times of trouble between them. During these times, the easy way out is to abandon each other.

Too, without being legally married a man and woman may feel and give very little respect to fidelity in the relationship. As the saying goes, "I'm not married to him, so why should I care," or "I'm not married to her, so why should I care."

So, in the end, the woman finds herself pregnant without a man who is willing to admit being father, and the man finds himself in the position of possibly facing a paternity suit and having to pay child support to a child in whom he disclaims any interest or responsibility.

Remember, while all states have paternity laws, a paternity suit is hard to prove, especially when the mother and the accused father are not legally living together at the time of the conception of the child. With the present philosophy of society in respect

---

[3]*U. S. News & World Report* (July 7, 1975) pp. 46-47.

to this matter, a judge or jury could easily infer in many cases that the woman could have had another man or men other than the alleged father, since, while living in such an arrangement, she is considered to have loose morals! Then there's also the burden of proving relationship in blood class, blood type, and physical characteristics between the alleged father and baby, and so on, to the exclusion of any other man possibly being involved other than the alleged father. This is quite a burden under these circumstances!

But most important in this type of situation is that the child may be born and grow up unwanted and neglected, with poor emotional growth and stability as the child attempts to meander through life, with little, if any, security provided by a mother and father.

On the other hand, when a man and woman go through the formal, legal procedure of becoming husband and wife in a marriage there's the feeling of mutual responsibility toward each other, a feeling of being faithful to each other, a feeling of mutually sharing problems of the marriage—not always, but more so than when living together without the ritual of a formal, legal marriage.

When living together in a legal marriage, the husband and wife are more apt to stick it out together when troubles come, more so than when living without the sanction of a legal marriage.

There are several reasons for this. First, they have been taught and internalized with making the marriage work. Secondly, there's a certain bit of social stigma attached to a separation or divorce, which is sometimes desirable to avoid.

Thirdly, no personal choice is theirs to irresponsibly abandon each other or their child or children because they are required to meet duties imposed by a court of law, if there's to be a divorce and sanctioned rights and duties. Of course, the court always is concerned with the welfare of a child when there's a division in a marriage, whether it be separation or divorce.

Unlike the living arrangement without a legal marriage, the husband is presumed by law to be the father of any child who is conceived during the legal marriage. Hence, if a legal marriage is to be dissolved, it must be done under requirements set forth in a court order. This does, to a large extent, provide protection to the father and mother and child when a division in a marriage occurs, whether it be separation or divorce. No such protection is available when there's no legal marriage.

As to communal living, the question arises as to whether or not a man and wife would have the privacy, the time together, and the attachment necessary in order to cement and keep together a faithful and responsible relationship in such living. There would be plenty of doubt in many cases, because, if a man and woman are to operate as a family, they must be free of outside influences. I'm wondering if this would be possible in communal living, unless everyone in the commune is to share and share alike, including the sharing of women and men!

Also, how could a child adequately identify with its parents in a commune? It would be rather difficult to do so. It appears, in our culture, anyway, that a child must be able to identify with the parents and look to the parents for love, affection, and care if the child is to attain normal and happy development. It's doubtful that this could be attained for a child in communal living because, in living under such conditions, the child would be deprived of attachment to its parents.

Equally as detrimental to a child's welfare as communal living is Ms. Steinem's theory, which is also the theory of the Movement, that a father should be equally responsible for the care of a child and that a mother should be equally afforded the opportunity and right to pursue a career outside the home, regardless of possible economic necessity. We'll have more about this in chapter 12 on child support, custody, and care.

Nor will we go into a discussion at this time on Ms. Steinem's theory that the traditional role of the wife will be no more, which is also the theory of the Movement, except to say that her theory on this would destroy a woman's image as a wife and her image of femininity and take away her longtime status as a person who has always been respected, admired, and protected by man, and, therefore, as a result of taking away the image of femininity, woman would lose many rights, gain none, which she has historically and traditionally enjoyed. We'll go into detail on these matters in later chapters.

However, we will mention at this time, with more to come in other chapters, that the Movement hopes to take away the image of femininity of a woman as an aim intended to do away with distinctions between man and woman. We'll see in chapter 7 that the image of femininity is woman's greatest virtue and power, and that, without it, she has little if anything going for her in relations with men.

Remember, the Movement has no quarrel with women in respect to their allegedly lowly status in life, but the contention of the Movement is that man is responsible for such status, and, therefore, the Movement's philosophy and actions are primarily directed at man.

Of course, the Movement has sought and is seeking to change the attitudes of women, which in turn is aimed at changing man's attitude according to the Movement's own specifications.

In other words, the Movement seeks to use women as tools in order to accomplish the Movement's objectives in relations with man.

At this point we may ask: Why not let men and women decide for themselves just how and what their personal relationship should and shall be? What is the Movement's real purpose in attempting to completely change structures in morality, religion, sexual relations, parent and child relations, relations in families, and relations in politics, economics, and relations in any and all other areas which may exist between man and woman?

Could it be that those in the Movement are unable to adjust to men, unable to adjust to marriage, unable to adjust to sexual relations, unable to adjust to family life, unable to adjust to children, and unable to adjust to other relations in society, and hope, therefore, that in some mysterious way and by some miracle that war against men will make them normal and happy persons?

Also, why do those in the Movement attack and label men and others who oppose the Movement and the ERA as male chauvinists, as unamerican, as opponents to change? In general, the Movement is radically resentful and bitter toward those who oppose its goals. Its intolerance is intensive and harsh and vindictive. The intolerance of the Movement directed at those who oppose the Movement's goals could easily be construed, and properly so, as being of jealous, envious, resentful, hateful, and undoubtedly anti-male.

All legitimate rights, such as equal employment opportunity, equal pay for equal work, and other rights of a legitimate nature are now well protected by laws without the need to have the ERA ratified, as we shall see in chapter 4.

The Movement's real aim is to have the ERA become law in order to use it as a tool to legally sanction and enforce its philosophy and actions which have to do with personal relations with man rather than legitimate legal rights in the social, economic, and political fields.

The ERA will be, if ratified and adopted as law, woman's worst enemy, setting her back for many years in good relations with man, as well as being bad for all other persons. Let's take a look in the next chapter at some of the predicted effects of the ERA if it should become law.

3

Legal Battles

If the ERA is ratified and adopted as law there'll be lawsuits and threats of lawsuits which will bring discord and chaos to the relations between husband and wife, to the relations between parent and child, to the relations among others in religion and in private business, and the ERA will take away the privacy of individuals, to mention only a few areas where the ERA will be disruptive to society.

All will be dismayed and far from happy with the ERA. Before going into the reasons, let us talk about the meaning of the ERA.

Really, no one knows its meaning. Uncertainty is as close as anyone can speculate as to its meaning. We can, however, predict what the nature of some lawsuits will be and what will be the effects of lawsuits on life.

Since the ERA will not become law until ratified by the required number of states, we're talking about a law that really doesn't exist. However, since it may very well become law, we need to look at some of the social, economic, and legal implications that will very likely affect relations between man and woman, between parent and child, between employer and employee, and among others which will likely arise from court decisions and legislation construing and interpreting and implementing the ERA, if and when it does become law.

The meaning and effects of the ERA will, if it becomes law, be primarily based on construction and interpretation given the ERA by the federal courts.

In predicting what the meaning and effects will be if it becomes law we can compare and contrast (by analogy as lawyers would do) the expected court decisions and expected implementing legislation of the ERA to what court decisions and implementing legislation have been in a similar body of law.

The most similiar body of law which we can compare and contrast to that of sex discrimination is that of race discrimination.

The federal courts have given force and interpretation for equality of rights based on race discrimination primarily under the "due process" and "equal protection" clauses of the Fourteenth Amendment to the U.S. Constitution. It would appear that these same clauses will be the primary tools for giving force and interpretation to equality of rights based on sex discrimination under the ERA, if it becomes law.

Powers of the courts in respect to decisions rendered in cases of race discrimination have been virtually unlimited. So, there's no reason to believe that the powers of the courts in respect to decisions rendered in cases of sex discrimination will be any less unlimited.

Nor has Congress been limited to any extent in finding powers needed to pass implementing legislation in the area of race discrimination, legislation commonly referred to as civil rights legislation. So, there's no reason to believe that Congress will be any less restricted in powers involving sex discrimination than it has been in powers involving race discrimination. Congress has always found immense powers under the "commerce" clause and under the "necessary and proper" clause of Article 1, Section 8 of the U.S. Constitution, when needed to pass civil rights legislation.

Legally speaking, the term "due process" means a sense of justice and sense of fairness, while the term "equal protection" means that the law protects one person to the same degree as it does another. The term "commerce" has been used to give Congress regulatory powers over any activity, whether interstate or purely local in nature, that has either a direct or an indirect effect upon the flow of interstate commerce, which includes such areas as civil rights, transportation, industry, agriculture, labor, and other areas of economic and social and political life. Under the "necessary and proper" clause Congress has used powers to carry out all enumerated powers of Congress under the U.S. Constitution. Like the powers of the courts, the powers of Congress are virtually unlimited, though many lawyers and many judges would disagree.

These terms have been used to give to Congress and to the federal courts virtually unlimited powers in nearly all areas of life, private as well as public. By far, the term "due process" has been the major weapon in the area of race discrimination, which also will be the major weapon in the area of sex discrimination.

We can't say that due process has resulted in a "sense of justice" and a "sense of fairness" or in "equality of rights" as a result of decisions handed down by the federal courts in the area of race discrimination. For example, if your son or daughter is forced to go to a school across town, against his or her will and against your will, then, the right to attend a school of choice is lost. Where is, then, the sense of justice or fairness or the sense of equal protection of law, if the right is lost simply because your son or daughter is of a particular race?

Too, if you have one hundred employees in your private business and you are ordered by the federal court to have at least thirty percent Black persons in your employment, then, where is the "sense of justice" and the "sense of fairness" or "equality of rights" under due process and under equal protection of the law, not only for you, but for the thirty whites who have lost their jobs to Blacks or for the whites who are qualified to work and whom you would hire, but can't, because they're white?

Look at a case which at the time of this writing is pending before the Fifth Circuit Court of Appeals in New Orleans, Louisiana. In this case a high school coach by the name of Billy Joe Adcox, a white man, who was assistant coach at Shreveport's Fair Park High in Louisiana, was appointed head coach at Southwood High. After receiving his first paycheck as the head coach, he was taken off the job by the Caddo Parish (County) School Board which gave as its reason, that his appointment was in violation of a federal court's desegregation order. The Board then appointed a Black man to position as head coach.

In this case, where is the "equal protection" or "due process"

of the law or the "equality of rights"? Didn't the court's order
clearly result in taking away the legal rights of one man and
giving them to another man, purely based on race? This seems
to be a clear case of inequality of rights, based on race discrimination, the very opposite of what equality of rights and equal
protection of the law are all about! No race discrimination should
legally mean that all races are treated equally under the law.
It certainly doesn't mean that a person of one race is given
preferential treatment under the law, to the detriment of a person
of another race!

Don't you suppose that there'll be inequality of rights based
on sex discrimination, should the ERA become law, making
"equal protection" and "due process" of the law, as well as
"equality of rights," a mere matter of deception?

So, like the laws for race discrimination, the laws for sex
discrimination will turn out to be, not a sense of justice and a
sense of fairness and not a sense of equal protection and not a
sense of equality of rights but a sense of injustice and a sense of
unfairness and a sense of inequality.

Of course, many who are opposed to the injustice and unfairness in the laws applicable to race discrimination are accused of
being racists, segregationists, and unamerican. Likewise, persons
who oppose the Movement and the ERA are and will be accused
of having links to the John Birch Society and to the Ku Klux
Klan. One such person is Phyllis Schlafty, a chief opponent of
the ERA and a leader of "Stop ERA" crusade.

It's quite common for opponents of a cause to be labelled and
smeared by the proponents of the cause as racist or Ku Klux
Klansman or as something else which sounds un-American.
Likely, some will give such labels to the author of this book
simply because he doesn't think that the Movement or the ERA
will advance equality of rights for women.

Now, let's go to the language of the ERA. The language is
simple enough and appears to be very American. It reads,
"Equality of rights under the law shall not be denied or abridged
by the United States or by any State on account of sex."

We can look to the language and point to certain words for

their expected meaning in an attempt to predict what the effects of the ERA will have on members of our society.

The word "equality" would seem to mean that both male and female must be afforded the same treatment under law. Yet, we know that this can't be true because of differences in circumstances involving occupations, differences in application of human efforts, differences in abilities, differences in economic and social goals which afford different opportunities, and differences in physical characteristics for man and woman.

In many instances, persons have never been treated the same under the law because of these differences.

Also, we know that, today, the law favors a person of a minority race over a person of the Caucasian race in many areas of life. For example, should a job with the government be available, a person of the minority race will get it, not the person of the Caucasian race. Also, today, women are hired before men, irrespective of qualifications in many instances, because of pressure from government officials. Unless women and minority groups are favored for jobs government funds will be withheld, as one example of pressure.

Yet we know that the person of the Caucasian race or the male may be as qualified, or more so, than the person of the minority race or the female. Then, where is the equality of rights? On the other hand, both white males and persons of the Caucasian race have had some advantages which the persons of the minority races and women have not had, until a few years ago.

For example, the "separate but equal" doctrine was lawful in public schools until the year 1954. Until then Blacks went to one school and whites went to another. Also, until recently, women were excluded from jobs primarily reserved for men, such as jobs in the military. In these cases, where is the equality of rights?

At best, the word "equality" is tossed around in the courts, meaning one thing today, something else tomorrow.

Let's look to other words in the proposed ERA. How about the words "United States" and "State"? They legally mean that rights cannot be "denied" or "abridged" by either the federal government or state governments. Legally this means that actions by private persons in private capacities will be excluded from the proposed ERA. But no one in the legal profession can take this legal distinction too seriously because the distinction has always been so much shibboleth and sham in the legal world.

For example, actions by private employers and private clubs have been held to be unconstitutional by the federal courts because the actions, though strictly private in nature, allegedly discriminated against persons of minority groups.

An employer who refuses to hire a Chinese or a Japanese or a Black or a member of any other minority group allegedly because of race will find himself in trouble with the law. Too, a private club which has to buy a county or a city license in order to operate will be in trouble with the law, should the club refuse to admit members of the minority races.

Also, if you or I refuse to sell our private home to a Chinese or to a Japanese or to a Black or to any member of the minority race allegedly for race reasons, we are in trouble with the law, though our actions are strictly private in nature.

These are only a few examples where supposedly the laws of race discrimination are to be applied to only government actions, but they equally apply to private actions. So, there's no reason to think that legal enforcement of alleged equality of rights in sex discrimination will apply only to federal and state actions.

If the ERA becomes law, its legal enforcement will pervade and tread on private life as well as on public life. Make no mistake about it!

While the words "equality" and "United States" and "State" are misleading and vague and ambiguous, yet the word "rights" is not only vague and ambiguous and misleading but is loaded with trickery! First, What rights? Second, whose rights? Third, to be denied or abridged by whom? Are we really talking about rights or an attempt by the Movement and proponents of the ERA to adjust all life in the relations between man and woman? Rights will turn out not to be rights but loss of rights and additional duties imposed on individuals! Every student of constitutional government knows this. However, the average citizen doesn't, and he should be told.

"Rights" are whatever the Supreme Court of the United States say they are. The Court may specify what rights are today, but they may be expanded or narrowed or taken away tomorrow.

Let's look to a few examples in history.

Rights of the people of various states to have the "separate but equal" doctrine for maintaining public schools for whites and Blacks existed from the time when the U.S. Constitution was adopted and finally ratified in the year 1789, until the year 1954, a period of one hundred sixty-five years. But, in the year 1954, the Supreme Court of the United States ruled, in the celebrated case of *Brown* v. *Board of Education*, et al, that the "separate but equal" doctrine constituted a denial of "due process," among others an alleged denial of rights under the Fourteenth Amendment to the U.S. Constitution. The ruling in this case held that the states could not keep and maintain separate schools for whites and Blacks for the intended purpose of segregation.

However, a few years later, the Court decided that "due process" meant not only that the states could not intentionally maintain segregation in public schools but also that it meant compulsory integration! Thus rights under "due process" were expanded for some and denied for others!

But this still was not enough to satisfy the court's thinking about the meaning of "due process." Hence its meaning was extended to "forced busing" in order to meet the requirement of compulsory integration. Too, the court has decided that parents cannot send their children to private schools, if to do so would hamper the process of speedy and compulsory integration.

In fact, the federal court in Miami, Florida has decided that private schools cannot refuse to be integrated. On May 29, 1975, U.S. District Judge Joseph Eaton ruled in Miami, Florida, that a church-related school, Dade Christian School, had to admit Black students.

Therefore, now, private schools, private businesses and private clubs as well as other private affairs must be integrated.

So, the only area which has not now been forced to be inte-

grated under federal court orders is the private home, all under
the guise of "due process" and "equality of rights," which law
was and is said to be applicable only to governmental actions!

If the private affairs of the people can be controlled and
governed by the federal courts acting under the guise of laws
governing race discrimination, why can't the people be further
controlled and governed in their private affairs under the guise
of laws governing sex discrimination? It can and will be done if
the ERA becomes law!

Thus the extension and expansion of rights for some and the
loss of rights for others under the guise of "due process" and
"equal protection" are a mysterious and never-ending road.

Just look at the turmoil in the schools of Boston, Massachusetts, today (September 15, 1975). So, What are private and
public rights of students and parents in schools? Whose rights?
Rights of Blacks or whites or both or neither? Likely, no one
knows! The same will be true for rights under the ERA if it
becomes law.

Rights have also changed from time to time in other areas
of the law. For example, under the Fourth Amendment to the
U.S. Constitution, the Supreme Court of the United States
maintained that illegal search and seizure applied only to federal
actions, from the time when the Amendment was adopted, in
the year 1791, until the case of *Mapp* v. *Ohio,* which was decided
in the year 1961. This was a sudden change in rights which had
existed for a period of one hundred seventy years. The ruling
in this case resulted in extending the meaning of "due process"
to state actions.

"Due process" of the Fourteenth Amendment was also extended to the right to counsel, court-appointed if necessary, in the
famous case of *Gideon* v. *Wainwright,* decided in the year 1963
by the U.S. Supreme Court, a right which did not exist for about
one hundred seventy-two years, but which came into being
under "due process."

The right to be warned of one's constitutional rights as funda-
mental to "due process" was handed down by the U.S. Supreme
Court in the case of *Miranda* v. *Arizona,* decided in the year

1966, but which right never before existed under "due process."

Voting has also come under the control and supervision of federal courts, pursuant to "due process." Until a few years ago, Congress and state legislatures had exclusive powers to construct voting districts for the purpose of voting. But suddenly the U.S. Supreme Court decided that it had jurisdiction under the U.S. Constitution to enforce the "one-man-one-vote" rule, in the name of "due process."

One may ask: If present rights under "due process" and "equal protection" of the U.S. Constitution are not definable or identifiable in scope and enforcement and that if these clauses apply to private as well as public (government) actions, how or why may one arrive at the conclusion that "rights" of the proposed ERA can be definable or identifiable and limited only to actions by the federal and state governments?

There's no reason to think that rights under the proposed ERA governing sex discrimination will be any more clear or definable and limited than is equality of rights governing race discrimination. Just as equality of rights under the law governing race discrimination is subject to construction and interpretation by the federal courts under "due process" and "equal protection," the same will be true for the law governing sex discrimination.

So, if one can't determine what the scope of rights or scope of loss of rights is, by looking to the language of the U.S. Constitution and to the court cases in respect to alleged race discrimination, then one can't be expected to know the scope of rights or scope of loss of rights by looking to the proposed ERA and to the predicted reasoning of court decisions in respect to sex discrimination.

At best, the proposed ERA and the predicted court decisions and implementing legislation will bring discord and chaos to man and woman, to parent and child, to private business and the privacy of individuals.

We don't need an amendment to the U.S. Constitution which we're told will mean one thing, but which will turn out to mean something else.

If we're to lose rights by the ERA, then we should be told,

and if the proposed ERA will adversely affect relations between husband and wife, between parent and child, and constitute an invasion of privacy, then the people who are expected to honor and obey the law have a right to know in order to defeat such a bad proposed law.

To afford any less to the people would be a breach of duty by Congress and the state legislatures whose members are, after all, servants of the people and who have the solemn duty to defeat such a law if it is not within the needs and happiness of the people.

Respect for law only comes with straight and forthright disclosure to the people who are to live with the law!

The people can't expect anything less than full disclosure of what the law is or will be. Nothing less than full and diligent examination and full disclosure in good faith of the consequences of the proposed ERA is acceptable to the people.

Nor should the people be misled with virtuous American words such as "equality" and "rights," when these terms are, in effect, "inequality" and "duties" intended to bring the people under more governmental restraint than already exists, restraint which will destroy happy and voluntary relations between man and woman, between parent and child, to say nothing about voluntary and workable relations between employer and employee.

Many women and many men who will be unhappy with marriage, unhappy with results of divorce proceedings, unhappy with home life, unhappy with employers, unhappy with social and economic conditions, and unhappy with other conditions in life will use sex discrimination as a means to vindicate themselves in whatever position is at hand. For example, a wife or a husband who doesn't receive what she or he thinks should be awarded in a divorce suit will yell, "sex discrimination!"

Accusations of sex discrimination will weave legal entanglements far and wide, in and around all areas of life. The ERA will, if ratified, be used as a weapon in order to justify the accusations. Some areas but only a few are as follows:

1. Divorce. A husband or wife who is in favor of a divorce

will be unhappy if a divorce is not granted by the court. The unhappy party will accuse the court and all concerned with unfairness because of discrimination based on sex. On the other hand, a husband or wife who is against a divorce being granted will accuse the court and all concerned with discrimination based on sex if a divorce is granted.

In every case the unhappy party to a lawsuit will attempt to prolong the legal grind, along with conflicts and tensions, by appealing to the appellate court for review of the trial court's decision. Legal fees, court costs, delays, and emotional strain will eat away at the parties to the lawsuit, stacking up hostility between man and woman while drawing in minor children to be used as tools for the purpose of allowing the mother and father to shoot poisonous hatred at each other.

2. Alimony. The wife who seeks alimony but doesn't receive it will be quick to accuse the court of taking the husband's side, based on sex discrimination, and the husband who has to pay alimony or pay too much in his opinion will accuse the court in showing favoritism to the wife, all in the name of discrimination based on sex.

3. Child custody. The mother or the father who doesn't gain permanent custody and control of minor children in lawsuits will accuse the court of conspiring with the other party, in violation of the ERA, all in the name of discrimination based on sex.

4. Visitation rights with minor children. In most cases, the party (usually the mother) who is awarded permanent custody and control of minor children in a divorce case must allow the other party (usually the father) certain days to visit with the minor children. What days for visitation and how many? Usually the mother or the father and sometimes both are unhappy with the days for visitation.

With the ERA in effect as a tool, the unhappy party or unhappy parties can continuously harass each other by filing for a change in visitations, all in the name of equal rights under the ERA.

5. Child support. The divorce court generally requires the father to pay a weekly or monthly sum of money to the mother

as support for minor children. Who should pay and how much? One may keep plugging away with the ERA as grounds for a lawsuit in order to find out. Harassment must go on!

6. Abortion. Some women are asking, "If a man isn't required to give birth to a baby, why should a woman?" Of course, the answer is that, once she has enjoyed sex, Mother Nature may see fit to make her pregnant, but not so for man.

The only thing that will make woman nearly equal to man in this respect is to have an abortion when becoming pregnant, unfettered by present legal requirements. Legal tests will come if and when the ERA becomes law.

7. Church. Some churches presently will not permit a woman to become a priest, a minister, or hold any other official position in the church because of religious beliefs. These beliefs can no longer be practiced should the ERA become law, because, under the ERA, a woman can hold any positions in church available to a man. There'll be a number of test lawsuits, if and when the ERA is fully ratified and adopted as law.

Official positions in church cannot be based on sex discrimination if the ERA becomes law.

Question: Will the First Amendment to the U.S. Constitution, which holds that neither the states nor the federal government can deny religious beliefs, have to be repealed if the proposed ERA (proposed Twenty-seventh Amendment to the U.S. Constitution) becomes law?

Certainly the First and proposed Twenty-seventh Amendments will be in conflict with each other. For the courts to tell a church that women (or men) must be able to hold official positions in a church is an infringement on religious beliefs.

To deny religious beliefs would be a major step in the destruction of our constitutional and democratic government.

8. Marriage. If a married man and a married woman can legally live together as husband and wife, free to indulge in sexual pleasures, how can an unmarried woman and an unmarried man be denied the same rights when the ERA becomes law, if it does?

Living together and sharing sexual pleasures can't be denied, based on sex discrimination!

Also, should the ERA become law, a woman can legally marry a woman or a man can legally marry a man. If a man can legally marry a woman or a woman can legally marry a man, why shouldn't a woman have the legal right to marry a woman or a man have the legal right to marry a man?

To deny choice of marriage based on sex will be in violation of the ERA if it becomes law!

9. Age. Women now receive many benefits at an earlier age than do men. With the ERA in force, a woman can't marry at an earlier age than can man and can't receive social security at an earlier age than can man, to name only a couple of instances where benefits are based on sex.

10. Other benefits based on sex. If and when the ERA becomes law, a widow who has never contributed to social security can't receive social security benefits when her husband dies, though she presently can, unless this same opportunity is afforded to a widower who presently doesn't have the right to receive social security benefits based on his wife's death.

Nor can women receive retirement benefits from companies at an earlier age than can men, though women do presently have this preferential treatment with many companies.

Economic benefits can't be based on sex discrimination under the ERA if and when it becomes law!

11. Homosexuality. A woman can engage in sex with another woman and a man can engage in sex with another man if and when the ERA becomes law because, with the ERA in effect, sexual pleasures cannot be restricted to acts between man and woman.

Choice of sex can't be based on discrimination of sex under the ERA!

12. Public accommodations. The barrier between man and woman in use of public accommodations, whether restroom or dressingroom or seating arrangement will have to go should the ERA become law. Some persons will test the distinctions pres-

ently being afforded man and woman in the use of public accommodations.

13. Public offices. If and when the ERA becomes law, women will want a pro rata share of offices, regardless of needs or qualifications or the will of the voters. Minority groups are being placed in offices by present court decisions and present bureaucratic agencies regardless of qualifications and equal opportunities for the majority. Why not afford the same preferential treatment to women under the ERA? Many women will be quick to find out by filing legal proceedings if and when the ERA becomes law.

14. Employer-employee. Under the ERA, many women will sue or threaten to sue for jobs, promotions, and additional salaries regardless of their qualifications or the needs of employers.

Some women will use the law of the ERA in order to receive "handouts" based on sex, just as many persons have used the law of race discrimination in order to receive "handouts."

"Either I get my way or I'll file a suit for discrimination," will become the thinking and action of many women, as it has become the thinking and action of many minority groups under the law of race discrimination.

Inequality, not equality, will become the order of the day!

15. Clothing and dress. What one wears in public, where it's worn in public, and how it's worn in public will become a single standard for both man and woman.

For example, if man can go topless on the beach or in a restaurant lounge, so can woman, under the ERA. If a girl or woman can wear hair down to her waist in school or in college or in church or at any other place, so can a boy or man.

There can't be discrimination in clothing and dress based on sex, if the ERA becomes law.

The ERA will be good news for many women as well as many proprietors who have been barred in some states from operating go-go "girlie" shows.

16. Husband and wife. Marriage, parent-child relations, and the family are the areas where the ERA will take its biggest and

most drastic toll in destroying our society as we now know it.

Personal quarrels between husband and wife will turn into legal battles with the ERA being used as a justifiable tool.

Strife between husband and wife will turn into divorce, disintegration of the family, improper care for minor children, and mental disorder for the father, for the mother, and for the child.

At this point, we can add a summary statement of what we've already said and what we'll say in the remaining chapters about the married woman: The ERA will have her locked into loss of custody of minor children in many cases, loss of alimony, loss of child support by the father in many cases, burdened with economic problems in supporting her minor children and supporting herself, loss of identity as a wife, and loss of femininity as a woman.

She will be the great loser, more than any other person, should the ERA become law. To some extent, the strong waves of the philosophy and actions of the ERA will engulf even the woman who is the most staunch anti-women's libber.

Lawsuits, legislation, and a way of life derived from the ERA will sweep and carry the woman who is an opponent of the ERA as well as the woman who is a militant supporter of it, if it becomes law.

Just as criminal laws must be obeyed by the innocent as well as the guilty, which has resulted in a way of life, so shall the ERA shape and mold society into its way of life for both opponents and proponents, should it become law.

The image of the single woman, the divorced woman, and the unhappily married woman, who are the most avid supporters of the ERA, will become the image of what society believes and what society will impose on the happily married woman, to some extent.

The good, the bad, the ugly, and the beautiful will be lumped together as a single standard for all women.

The single standard will grow and become more standardized as the legal battles rage on and on. Indeed, every disagreement between man and woman, in all areas of life, can, and will, in many cases, turn into legal battles in the name of equal rights under the ERA, and the Promised Land for Women shall become a land of discord and chaos.

To be sure, the restless, the agitators, and the maladjusted ones who hope to promote the ERA will find encouragement, breadth, and growth in the federal courts, where the legal battles will be fought in the event that the ERA becomes law.

Federal courts have been ever ready and thirsty to extend their powers of control into state and local affairs and into the privacy of schools and individuals, in the name of race discrimination and in the name of "due process" for civil rights, good labor, good industry, good agriculture, and good business, to name only a few areas. The courts will be equally thirsty to inject themselves into private affairs in the name of equality of rights based on sex.

Let's briefly discuss a few areas, some of which we have already mentioned:

1. Voting. The federal government now pretty much controls voting for both federal and state offices. Not only do the federal courts require "districting" based on criteria suitable to the notions of the federal courts, all in the name of "due process" and "equal protection" of law, but federal officials now watch over the voter's shoulders at voting booths under the guise of the federal Voting Rights Act.

These are areas which at one time were considered to be powers belonging to the people and to the states, until the federal courts and Congress decided to have a juggling of rights!

If the federal courts and Congress with their civil rights legislation can invade the privacy of citizens' rights to vote and invade the powers of the states to control voting, in the name of "due process," so, don't you think that these centralized authorities can invade the privacy between man and woman in the home and in other places under the ERA, all in the name of "due process"?

2. Race discrimination. If the federal courts under "due process" and under "equal protection" of the law can require compulsory integration in both private and public schools, forced busing, compulsory integration of private employment, com-

pulsory integration of private clubs, compulsory integration of residential living by controlling the sale of private homes—areas once beyond the constitutional powers of the federal courts— along with Congress' implementing legislation on civil rights, then, certainly, we can expect the federal courts and Congress to further invade the privacy between man and woman under the "due process" and "equal protection" of the law under sex discrimination pursuant to the ERA if it becomes law.

3. Criminal laws. Under the doctrine of police powers, health, morals, and public welfare have been considered to be powers solely for the states under the U.S. Constitution. Thus about all crimes were, until not too long ago, within the exclusive jurisdiction of the states. However, the federal courts have steadily and diligently chipped away at the states' police powers so that, today, about all state criminal prosecutions are subject to federal court review, pursuant to "due process."

Also, Congress has been busy usurping powers of the states and individuals with such enactments as the civil rights laws and with regulatory laws over individuals and private business under the guised authority purportedly in the "commerce" clause and in the "necessary and proper" clause within Article I, Section 8, of the U.S. Constitution.

Today, the states and individuals have very few rights that are not subject to control by the federal courts and Congress.

While the three areas mentioned above certainly do invade individual privacy, yet they are not as far-reaching as invasion of individual privacy will be if the ERA becomes law.

True, the federal court decisions on race discrimination do affect the rights to privacy for many persons, but these paternalistic and dictatorial decisions have not yet marched up the front doorsteps, into the living room, then into the bedrooms of private homes, as will be the case under the decisions rendered pursuant to the ERA, if and when it becomes law.

This is so, because the ERA will eventually affect, either directly or indirectly, nearly every man and woman and every boy and girl and their marital and family relations, since every male and every female is either a husband or wife or hopes to be, someday, with the exception for those who have already been in this status.

Private as well as public disputes between male and female are potential lawsuits, to be based on sex discrimination.

Thus the far-reaching effects of the ERA on man and woman, on parent and child, and on family affairs, as well as economic and social affairs will be subject to control and invasion by the federal courts and implementing legislation of Congress.

No need to be taken in by the arguments of the promoters and supporters of the ERA, that the laws of the ERA will include only limited actions of the state and federal governments, then only when such actions are discriminatory, based on sex. This has not been true for a predicted similiar and analogous body of law, race discrimination.

For example, would you have believed in the year 1954 when the Supreme Court of the United States handed down the case of *Brown* v. *Board of Education, et al*, that this decision would have been stretched to include federal control over the make-up of students, make-up of teachers, types of school songs, types of school symbols, "forced busing," and overall dictatorial supervision of schools by federal courts, as well as control of whom employers shall employ in private business, which employees shall be hired by the governments, which members shall be admitted to a private club, and to whom you may sell your private home? Likely not, but it is safe to say that decisions rendered pursuant to the ERA, if and when it becomes law will have more far-reaching effects than have decisions rendered pursuant to the laws involving alleged race discrimination.

The exception is that control of individuals by the federal courts and Congress, in respect to sex discrimination, will intrude into individual privacy of husband and wife, into privacy of parent and child relations, and into privacy of the home, since laws of sex discrimination will be applicable to all persons. On the other hand, while control of individuals through manipulation of laws in respect to race discrimination is broad, it doesn't include all persons, because the courts and Congress have not, as yet anyway, attempted to control private actions and relations of husband and wife and relations of parent and child which are directed toward each other in the privacy of the home.

It wouldn't be easy for a husband or a wife to accuse and sue each other based on race discrimination. However, each may very well accuse and sue the other for alleged sex discrimination under the laws of the ERA!

The proponents of the ERA may say, "Oh, well, the federal court decisions or legislation of Congress will only decide the issue of sex discrimination, nothing more!"

Not so! For example, when the federal courts have decided constitutional issues of a state criminal case, they have, in effect, controlled and decided all aspects of the case. When the federal courts have decided issues of race discrimination in school cases, they have, in effect, taken firm control of the entire general operations of the schools, in many cases. The far-reaching effects in the control of human affairs resulting from court decisions involving sex discrimination will be no less restrictive than is true of court decisions involving race discrimination.

Too, when Congress has passed legislation governing civil rights or regulation of private commerce, it has gained control over individuals and businesses. In effect, Congress has said, "Either you do it our way, or you face both prosecution and cutting off of federal funds."

The same reasoning will apply to the application of laws passed and decided pursuant to the ERA, label the expected actions of the courts and Congress whatever you choose!

Let's take the federal law on sex education passed in the year 1972 for the alleged purpose of ending sex discrimination in schools and colleges. President Ford sent to Congress on June 3, 1975, through his Secretary of Health, Education, and Welfare, Mr. Caspar Weinberger, new sweeping rules which are to be applied to all schools and colleges which receive federal funds, and this includes most schools and colleges in the nation. The rules are intended to broaden existing federal powers over activities of schools and colleges.

Take a look at some of the controlling aspects of the proposed rules. Generally, they require equal treatment of the sexes in respect to admissions, classroom instruction, after-school activities, sports, housing, employment in education, and payments of federal funds.

But the law will be much broader than the general provisions. For example, it includes a proposal requiring state and local officials and others to allow pregnant girls to attend classes; a provision would make pregnancy, childbirth, false pregnancy, and abortion only temporary disabilities to girls, with no penalty to be applied by the schools and colleges; a provision disallowing separate curfew hours for females; a provision requiring gym classes to be sexually integrated, and sex quotas for medical and law schools, to name only a few of the specific provisions.

You can see that these provisions have nothing to do with equality of rights or with qualifications of students or with their abilities or with their desires or with quality education. The enforcement of these provisions will result in compulsory integration of the sexes, nothing more!

The theory is that a school or college which does not adhere to the provisions will be denying "equality of rights" under "equal protection" of the law and under "due process" of the law.

Sex discrimination under the federal act is another example where the federal government is playing Big Brother with the rights and the money which belong to the people, a sample, but more extensive role which the federal government will play under the ERA, if it becomes law.

And there'll be no end to the role played by the federal government in invading the rights of privacy for individuals. Agitators of the Movement, coupled to Congress and federal courts which seek extension of their awesome powers over the control of individuals will be a never-ending process.

Already, without waiting for ratification of the ERA as authority or for any other authority, the National Organization of Women (NOW) has included demands in its platform for federalized enforcement of support orders and child custody decrees governing lawsuits between husband and wife.

Already, without waiting for ratification of the ERA as authority or for any other authority, the U.S. Senate has been considering the demands of NOW in Senate Bill Number 2081. Any good lawyer knows that the demands include areas of authority which belong only to the states, and this is the way it should be, because the state legislatures and state judges are at local levels, familiar with laws which govern local affairs which affect local families and their local needs.

Federal control over the private affairs of individuals will go on unless stopped. The ERA will, if it becomes law, give federal courts and Congress control of the one main remaining area presently free of centralized federal control, privacy of the home.

Remember, judges and members of the Congress and members of state legislatures, as well as Governors, are servants of the people, and, as such, should be responsive to the will and needs of the people. Therefore, invasion into the privacy of the people can be stopped! Unless these elected officials will enact laws which serve the needs and happiness of the people, then elect those who will.

How about federal judges? They also can be controlled in order to serve the needs and happiness of the people. In order to understand this, let's look briefly at the structure and powers of the federal court system.

The only court created by the U.S. Constitution is the Supreme Court of the United States. All others (federal courts) are created by Congress, pursuant to authority granted to Congress under Article I, Section 8, of the U.S. Constitution.

The Supreme Court of the United States has very limited authority where cases can be filed with it and decided by it. Nearly all of its authority is by way of review of cases which originate in the trial courts, the federal district courts. Cases which originate in the trial courts are appealed to the Circuit Court of Appeal, then to the U.S. Supreme Court.

Without authority to review cases which originate in the trial courts (federal district courts) the United States Supreme Court would no longer have authority to decide cases involving sex discrimination, race discrimination, or any other type of case which we've mentioned.

As Congress has the power to create the federal district courts and the Circuit Courts of Appeal, it also has the power to abolish these courts, which would cut off all appellate review authority for the United States Supreme Court. Hence Congress could do one of three things in order to curb decisions which are unfavorable to the will and needs of the people: first, it could abolish the federal district and circuit appeals courts; second, it could limit the kind of cases which can be appealed to the U.S. Supreme Court; thirdly, it could limit the nature of cases which could be filed in the trial courts (federal district courts).

A fourth measure by Congress would be more appropriate and less drastic in action. Presently, federal judges of the trial courts and the courts of appeal are appointed to office for life, subject to removal only by impeachment proceedings. Congress could amend statutory law, making judges of these courts run in an election for office, just as the President of the United States does or as members of state legislatures do or as members of Congress must do, as well as Governors of all the states.

Some judges, if not all, would be more responsive to the will and needs of the people if they had to gain office by being elected by the people.

So, the people do have a remedy, if they think that the ERA will be bad law or it turns out to be bad. Of course a remedy still available is that the ERA can be repealed if and when it becomes law, just as the Prohibition Amendment was repealed.

If it becomes law, the ERA will pit wife against husband, and husband against wife, and it will result in tearing down the walls of security for minor children, not to mention loss of freedom in such areas as the home, the schools, private business, and religion.

With the ratification and adoption of the ERA, liberal federal judges and a liberal Congress, both thirsty for extending their powers into the privacy of individuals as well as into the general processes of economic and social life, coupled with agitation of the Movement, legal battles will shake to the ground marriages, relations between husband and wife, relations between parent and child, relations in religion, relations between employer and employee, and relations in the family institution.

The proposed ERA is a proposed law which we don't need. We already have sufficient laws governing sex discrimination, as we'll see in the next chapter.

4

Adequate Law Without the ERA

Is there a need for the ERA to become law? Only if there are not existing legal rights for women which afford adequate legal protection. Men in general are not asking for ratification and adoption of the ERA as law.

First, there must be some limitation in area placed on the scope wherein legal rights exist, and the scope must be legally reasonable in number and kind of rights. Secondly, the legal rights must be definable in order to reasonably answer our question.

A woman is, as well as a man, entitled to legal rights for only legitimate purposes. For example, such purposes do not extend to all personal relations between a husband and wife. These persons can agree to where they will live, how they will live, how and where they will rear their children, whether or not the wife will retain her maiden name, whether or not the wife or the husband or both will pursue careers outside the home, all without laws.

These personal relations cannot be legislated or litigated with an end to making a husband and wife or relations between a single woman and a single man happy. Either these persons must be free to decide for themselves without restraints by law on these matters or go their separate ways.

If they can't mutually agree, then they have legal remedies in the divorce court, or in some other court, or they may choose to live together without reaching amicable agreements on these matters. Whatever decision in respect to personal relations is made must be by personal choice, not by legal compulsion. Law can't compel a man and a woman to exist in a happy relationship!

In short, the personal affairs of the home, sex life between a man and woman of the home, personal happiness or unhappiness between a man and woman, and the personal affairs between a parent and child are not legitimate purposes which can be controlled or compelled by law. Of course, all states have laws to protect all persons against abusive and violent acts which have nothing to do with equal rights, such as laws on divorce and crimes.

Keep in mind that no laws compel a woman and man to live together or work together, which is the way, and properly so, that our society allows a man and woman to choose freely and formulate good relations.

Legal coercion has never and will never result in forming a happy relationship between man and woman, between parent and child, and among those who choose freely to associate.

Nor is the personal and social association with all individual persons or groups an area which warrants legal sanction. For example, if a person doesn't like the Baptist Church and its doctrines, then he can join the Methodist or the Catholic or some other church. Nor is a person legally to be accepted or employed as a member in every profession, in every business, or in every civic organization, simply because he or she happens to be of a particular sex.

Also, a person of a particular sex is not legally entitled to a job in a particular field simply because he or she is of a particular sex.

Our society places certain restrictions on its members in order to maintain social control of the members for the benefit of society as a unitary body. Therefore, neither woman nor man will ever be able to use sex as a tool for arriving at all personal goals, at least in an organized and democratic society which considers the legal rights of all persons, not only the rights of persons of a particular sex, ethnic group, religion, or race.

To grant unlimited rights to one person or to one group would be to deny rights to another person or to another group. Well applicable is the theory that one person's rights end where the next person's rights begin. Of course, this theory must be practiced if it is to be meaningful.

Hence, the Movement can't expect to be granted unlimited legal rights for women based on sex. Nor can the Movement expect to have its beliefs codified by the ERA as rules of law to be imposed on everyone else!

Somewhere and somehow all legal rights must be defined if they are to be recognized and respected, and the scope of the legal rights must be reasonable in area.

Laws in our society are enacted and enforced for the purpose of giving reasonable protection to persons and property. In other words, legal protection doesn't give a woman the right, simply because she is a woman, to engage in every economic or every professional activity occupied by a man, or to occupy any and every religious, social, and political position occupied by a man. Nor does one man have the legal right to occupy and enjoy every position occupied and enjoyed by another man, unless earned and accepted, based on capabilities.

So, a woman is, as a man is, entitled to legal rights which are definitive and limited in scope and also reasonable.

It is submitted that she now has these rights which cannot be discriminated against based on sex, and that there is no need for the passage of the ERA in order to give to her all the legal rights to which she is entitled.

For example, in its term ending June 30, 1975, the Supreme Court of the United States ruled that employers cannot discriminate against women in the respect to wages for the same work performed by both men and women. Women must be given the same pay as men. It also ruled that mandatory maternity leave at a set time in pregnancy violates due process of the U.S. Constitution.

In addition, the Court ruled that women must be given equal opportunity to serve on juries, as an equal protection of the law; the Court declared a Utah law, which provided the age of majority for females to be eighteen and males to be twenty-one, unconstitutional because it violated the equal protection provided by the Constitution.

Thus, laws which discriminate against women based on sex are now, it appears, in violation of the due process and equal-protection clauses of the U.S. Constitution.

Therefore, the ERA will not serve any legitimate purpose in respect to alleged discrimination based on sex, since such discrimination is prohibited by the U.S. Constitution, without the ERA.

In addition to the rulings of the U.S. Supreme Court, Congress has passed laws doing away with discrimination based on sex. The Equal Pay Act of 1963 was applied to a case in the U.S. Supreme Court on June 3, 1974. In this case, against Corning Glass Works, the Court ruled that women cannot be discriminated against in respect to wages for the same work performed by them as performed by men. Women must be given the same pay as men for the same work; so said the Court.

Under the Equal Credit Opportunity Act, lending institutions are required to make credit equally available to credit-worthy customers, without regard to sex or marital status.

Too, Congress has approved an act allowing women to be admitted to the military academies. In fact, women are now entitled to equal opportunities with men in the military services.

Under the Women's Education Equity Act, women are afforded equal rights with men in respect to educational opportunities.

Not only do the federal authorities grant equal rights to women but a majority of the states now have laws doing away with discrimination based on sex, and the states which may have laws upholding sex discrimination are likely to find that such laws are unconstitutional in light of the rulings of the U.S. Supreme Court.

One must now conclude that there is no law which can legally discriminate against women based on sex, and that women now have full legal protection against discrimination in areas which warrant legal sanction.

Not only do women now have all legal rights afforded to men, but they have more than men. Women are now given preferential treatment in applications for jobs with federal and state governments. Governmental agencies are seeking quotas for jobs to be filled by women.

For example, a former colleague of mine who taught at a college with me applied for a position in teaching at another college in Florida. At the time he had a Ph.D. degree in history and all the qualifications needed for the position which the college was seeking to fill, but he was told that the position had to be filled by a Black person or by a woman, preferably by a Black woman. He didn't get the position.

Thus, we already have reverse discrimination in sex, against men and in favor of women in many areas, especially in governmental positions.

The U.S. Department of Health, Education, and Welfare has demanded and is demanding that groups which receive federal funds must increase employment for women; else, funds will be withheld.

Although we have adequate laws to do away with discrimination based on sex, where it exists, yet the Women's Liberation Movement insists that it is imperative to ratify and adopt the ERA as law. Publicly, the reason given by the Movement is that the ERA will allow the courts to treat sex as a "suspect classification" which is the manner in which the courts have treated race in alleged cases of race discrimination.

Just what does "suspect classification" mean? In cases involving alleged race discrimination it has meant, in reality, that, when a person of a minority race has been denied or refused a demand, such denial or refusal was presumed to be based on race discrimination. For example, a refusal to sell a home to a Black person has automatically been presumed to be because the person was Black.

In other cases, where a person of a minority race has been denied employment, the automatic presumption has been that the denial was based on race discrimination.

Therefore, the Women's Liberation Movement seeks to use the same modus operandi through the ERA that the Civil Rights Movement has used under the equal-protection and due-process clauses of the U.S. Constitution.

Where minority persons or minority groups have met with denials or refusals in their demands they have been, in many cases, quick to file lawsuits or to file complaints with governmental agencies or both, alleging that such denials or refusals were based on race discrimination.

The suggested aim of the Women's Liberation Movement is to use the ERA as a tool to file lawsuits or complaints with agencies based on sex discrimination when women are met with denials or refusals, should the ERA become law.

But the Movement doesn't need the ERA to pursue such aim. This aim can be pursued by way of the equal- and due-process clauses of the U.S. Constitution, as has been done by the Civil Rights Movement. These are the clauses which the courts have used to compel integration, to compel forced busing, to compel job priorities for minority groups or persons, and to compel other remedies for minorities. There's no reason to believe that the courts will not use these clauses, as they have already done in some cases, to end alleged sex discrimination.

This leads to the question, What is the real aim of the Women's Liberation Movement in seeking passage of the ERA? The suggested answer is that the Movement hopes to use the ERA as a tool in taking a shotgun approach to changing the entire structure of human relations.

It is suggested that the Movement sees the ERA as being so sweepingly broad in powers so that any and every possible grievance of women can be petitioned in a court of law.

By using the ERA as a tool, the Movement hopes to do away with all distinctions in identities which exist between man and woman. For example, the Movement seeks to do away with the customary and traditional roles of husband and wife, do away with the customary and traditional roles between parent and child, do away with customary and traditional roles in sex life, do away with customary and traditional roles in marriage and divorce, to mention only a few of the expectations sought by the Movement through the proposed ERA.

Really, the Movement's quest for changes is primarily in the field of personal relations between man and woman. The quest has very little if anything to do with legitimate purposes in having laws to reasonably protect woman's person and property.

The Movement's expectations in changes are psychological, not legal! Thus solutions to such changes must be found in the person, not in a court of law or before a governmental agency.

The happiness or unhappiness which may exist in personal relations between man and woman is strictly voluntary, and therefore legal compulsion through the ERA will not cure the ills in such relations.

In order to change such states between man and woman, the man and woman must be free and willing to seek proper and personal adjustments. Desirable adjustments cannot be compelled by law.

The ERA would, if passed as law, only serve as a tool to further agitate, irritate, and frustrate relations between man and woman. In the end, the ERA would only result in making matters worse in the woman's world.

5

Woman's World

As a wife or as a woman who has an intimate male friend, do you like for him to do the following:

To bring flowers to you on special occasions, at times such as anniversaries, birthdays, and Christmas?

To hold your hand when crossing a busy street?

To open your car door when getting in a car?

To proudly introduce you to guests on social occasions?

To give his seat to you when you are having to stand?

To pull out your chair and seat you when you're in a plush restaurant for dinner?

To acknowledge your presence at a social gathering by rising when you enter the room where the gathering is being held?

To light your cigarette, especially when you are attending a social function?

To open the door at home when you arrive after an evening out?

To let you enter first when entering church, when entering a restaurant, when entering a friend's home, or when entering into his or your car?

To tip his hat to you or to other women when you see him downtown or when with him downtown?

To pay your expenses when you're out being entertained for dinner or for any other social occasion?

To change a flat tire on your car?

To allow you to be served first, before him, at a cocktail party or when out having dinner?

To assist in taking your coat off after entering a room and to assist in securing it and placing it on you when leaving the room?

To protect you from improper advances and from abuses from others when out for the evening?

To hold you in his arms on a cold night when outside?

To dress himself sharply when out with you at a formal dance or at a formal banquet?

To assist you in preparing for travel, such as running errands to the airlines or depot office for your ticket?

To carry your baggage for you or to carry those things for you which may be a little too heavy for you?

To gently hold you and gently kiss you when leaving you and when returning to you?

To caress you, especially in times of sorrow or in times of sadness?

To assist you at times when you are tired at work or when your burdens seem heavy?

To protect you from wrongdoings by others to you?

To feel wanted and loved by him?

To feel needed and secure in his presence?

Be honest! What are your answers? If your answers are yes, or if a majority of your answers are yes, then we can assume that you do like the special courtesies and the special place that man believes, and which you believe, that a woman should have in our society.

In short, you want to be treated like a woman and a lady!

Your man wants and expects you to have a special place in his life. You're special to him, and you always will be, unless you do something to change his feelings for you. You are first and foremost in his life, and you always will be unless you let your actions and philosophy interfere with your relations to him.

Don't let the actions and philosophy of the Movement and the proposed ERA take away your special place with your man!

Those little things which your man does for you or what he says to you is his way of recognizing you as a person of feminine beauty, a loving and charming wife and woman. You're a special person in our society, and he recognizes this. He reflects an attitude which is internalized in our society.

You have been placed on a pedestal because you're a woman, a person of femininity, a person who represents the most of beauty in Creation.

Your world is a position of distinction which you have, a distinction between man and woman. Your beauty, your charm, your special place in society, your femininity, and your towering presence among men are your world, a world occupied only by you, and a world which will last and endure only by your philosophy and actions.

Honor and Admiration and Respect walk in hand with you in your world.

Can you think of one mature and well-adjusted woman who doesn't like this world?

Don't let the philosophy and actions of the Movement and the proposed ERA destroy it for you. Ask yourself, What would be my world if I didn't have the special recognition which is given to me by man and society?

As a woman, you are revered, worshiped, and admired by man. You are courted, loved, and protected by him. His attitude and actions are a way of life toward woman in our society. It's social attitude which prevails toward woman. To have this attitude is considered to be good taste. To have good manners, to be a man of good breeding, a man of gentility are part of an attitude, some call *chivalry*.

Chivalry arose with the ideals and practices of the knightly class of the Middle Ages. The word chivalry is derived from the French word *cheval*, meaning horse. Back in the Middle Ages, knights rode on horses. The knights were loyal to superiors, and courteous, kind and gentle to the weak.

The chivalrous code is respect, reverence, and admiration for women, which code, though unwritten, is still a part of man's attitude toward woman, especially in the Western world. It certainly has existed in the United States.

Chivalry is certainly complimentary to woman, and not the least bit degrading to her, as some would have you think. For example, some in the Movement have taken a negative attitude toward chivalry, based on my observations. It's quite true that once the pedestal on which woman is placed by man is removed, the distinction between her and him will disappear. This is the very thing which some hope will happen!

If this should happen, what would be woman's world? As a woman, count your gains and your losses and compare them, if the distinction should disappear.

Without respect and protection of the status which woman has enjoyed, the status will no longer exist. The status is only as strong as the respect and faith held by man for it. It consists of man's attitude toward woman, which is nothing more than good courtesy, favorable compliments, decorum, proper etiquette, honor, gallantry, and generally good manners toward woman.

No woman who is mature and well-adjusted objects to these things. On the contrary, they are cherished by her. Such an attitude by man toward woman is expected by woman.

Not only is it expected by woman but perhaps by all of our society. A man who doesn't have such an attitude is thought to be crude, uncouth, reprehensible, and anything but a gentleman!

He is held responsible for proper and courteous recognition of woman. Therefore, the Movement and the proposed ERA offer to women the following: Loss of good recognition for her, which is the very thing which the Movement and supporters of the ERA hope to have. It won't come, however, when the Movement and the ERA destroy the attitude which has held the recognition for woman.

Should her world of recognition which exists in the distinctions between man and woman be destroyed, it'll be done by her own philosophy and actions, and not by man!

No doubt, a vast majority of men as well as a vast majority of women approve of and like the pedestal on which woman is perched.

You've seen men extend special courtesies to women, such as allowing a woman to enter a restaurant first or any other place, holding the door for her to enter, assisting her when she has car trouble, giving his seat to her on a crowded bus or train, to name only a few courtesies extended to her, but have you ever seen a man extend these courtesies to another man?

Likely not, and likely you will not, because man lets another man pretty much fend for himself. However, even a man who is a stranger to a woman will see that the woman is afforded reasonable conveniences, if it is within his control to do so.

How and by what means may you as a woman lose this world of yours, a world in which you, in effect, enjoy a special and protected status?

It's simple, because all you have to do is to change your role and your attitude toward man. All you have to do is to insist that you compete with a man in his world, and he'll soon treat you as if you were a man. All you have to do in order to change is to think change, talk change, act change, represent change; then there'll be change!

So, if you change to a man's world, what have you gained for yourself? Certainly you will not have any more legal rights, but fewer rights, as this book points out. Such will be the case, if and when the ERA becomes law.

How about your losses, if and when the ERA becomes law? First, you lose your world of respect and admiration from man when the law starts grinding and your demands are felt, along with your loss of femininity and identity as a wife and woman, which we shall later discuss. Certainly, under the ERA, you will have to fend for yourself in the economic world, without any special consideration from man.

You see, when your attitude toward yourself and your attitude toward man change in accordance with the philosophy and actions of the Movement, then his attitude toward you will change. When it does, the pedestal on which you have been placed will cease to exist. No law such as the ERA can keep this from happening.

Man will treat you now, as well as forever, just as you ask to be treated. You will receive from him just what you ask for. Ask to be treated like a man, and so it shall be! Ask for loss of the courtesies extended to you by man and society, and it shall be done! As in other areas of life, so as in your relations to man; you as a woman shall reap what you sow.

Many of those in the Movement as well as many who support the ratification of the ERA are acting in good faith, but they may have little or no understanding of what will happen to women by their philosophy and actions. Still, there are many who support the Movement and the ERA, who would like to see drastic changes in woman's relations to man, as well as her relations in marriage, in divorce proceedings, in the family, at work, or wherever she may be.

The latter group of supporters and proponents of the ERA seems to be saturated with frustration intended to be released on man. It's man who is responsible for their sorry plight and unhappiness in life; so they seem to think. Therefore, they have chosen man as their target, not realizing that woman may be her only enemy, not man. Woman's success or lack of success in life is dependent primarily on her attitude of herself.

Yet, in order to release themselves from what they call oppression by man, suppression by man, injustice by man, the Movement now stages a crusade in the name of equal rights for women, which will turn out to be anything but equal rights.

The crusade includes a number of strategic and tactical maneuverings, one of which is to lead you, as a woman, to believe that the man who is chivalrous toward you is about to exploit you, through trickery or deceit. There's no proof of this, nor is there likely ever to be.

Another accusation is that the person who opposes the Movement and the ERA is chauvinistic, which merely means having unreasonable loyalty to an ideal or cause, being opposed to change.

Change, for woman, is good, if the change will advance her welfare and happiness. However, the changes for woman produced by the philosophy and actions of the Movement, to be worsened by the ERA if it becomes law, are changes which are against her interests. For example, loss of the image of femininity, loss of her identity as a respected and admired wife, loss of alimony, loss of child support, along with other losses mentioned in this book are not changes which will advance the interests of woman.

Of course, one main accusation within the tactics and strategies of some who support the Movement and the ERA is the one which accuses a person who opposes the ERA as being un-american, that no one can possibly oppose equality of rights and still be American. Such is an erroneous and deceptive argument, as we've seen in chapter 3.

The philosophy and actions of the Movement will, if adopted and practiced, strip you of your womanhood.

You, as a woman who loves and approves of chivalry and the courtesies of society for woman, may very well be accused by the Movement of accepting a degrading and subordinate role in relation to man. Reason and logic, along with an application of common sense for your world, will teach otherwise. Without the anti-woman philosophy preached by the Movement, and without laws such as the ERA which will strip you of your world of femininity, you will continue to have your world of love, respect, and admiration.

You reign as one who is special to man in your world of femininity. You have rank which is more than that afforded to him. You as a woman are protected and pursued by man. You'd rather be sought and pursued by man than used in a mercenary way and then rejected by him!

Because of your special place in relation to man, you're always sought by him. However, should the philosophy and actions of the Movement and the laws of the ERA take away your distinctions of femininity by changing man's attitude to your world, you'll likely be used by him, not cherished and pursued by him.

If only woman is to be injured by destroying her world of femininity, why should man be concerned? Because an injury to woman is also an injury to man.

Man and woman live together, and they happily live together only when working together, not when working in opposite directions. One can't pull while the other pushes. For woman to strip herself of femininity is to deprive man of what he most cherishes, a very feminine and beautiful woman.

There can be no beauty in woman without femininity. Her feminine appearance, her feminine mannerisms, and her feminine touch are all based on her relation to man in a culture such as ours which teaches her to be feminine.

In this culture of ours, man doesn't expect woman to be a mere robot. I'm convinced that a vast majority of men want a woman to be and to do whatever makes her most happy, within our moral and ethical code. This includes change in woman, change in her philosophy of life, change in her relation to man if necessary. Standing still in life accomplishes nothing!

However, the main thing is this: he expects and desires that she retain her femininity. Change in a woman's outlook on life, change in her occupation, and change in other areas of life don't necessarily mean that such changes will result in loss of her femininity.

On the other hand, when woman attempts purposely to engage in activities which are normally considered to be masculine, then we have another situation. Her attempts to compete with man in masculine activities for the mere sake of showing him that she can legally do so will lessen her femininity. You are seen to be that which you think, feel, and act. Let's take an extreme example. A woman in man's clothes, doing a man's job in a lumber yard certainly detracts from her femininity. If she keeps this up long enough, she'll develop the manners of men around her, and pretty soon no one will think of her as a person of femininity.

Woman's attempts to abandon the traditional work in her home purposely in order to work in the same places and under the same conditions as those under which her husband or man works, for the mere sake of competing with him, prove nothing for her femininity!

In order to teach man a lesson, the Movement and the supporters of the ERA are staging, in effect, an anti-feminine crusade. No lesson is necessary because man already knows that a woman is far superior to man in those things which naturally fit within her world of femininity. For example, the beauty of a woman is far superior to the beauty of a man in most ways.

The anti-feminine crusade will do nothing but take away a woman's world of femininity. Then what will she have left?

Let woman reach for the stars! Man doesn't mind. So long as she can be happy, she'll make her husband or man happy.

But, an attempt to force man to change his attitude of woman through the law proposed by the ERA will do nothing for woman, except likely drive a wedge further between her and him, not only making her more unhappy but also doing the same for man.

Such law will merely change the attitude of woman toward man and the attitude of man toward woman. In the process, man will lose his image of femininity for woman.

Let's face it, the world of femininity is an attitude held by man as to the image of woman, based on woman's actions and philosophy, and not an attitude held by one woman for another woman. Take all the men out of woman's world, then would she really care as to whether or not she had a world of femininity?

Yet, not a woman wants to lose her world of femininity, should the truth be known. Ask any woman, "Do you want to be treated and respected as a woman?" You know the answer!

Whether or not she will continue to be treated and respected as a woman in her world of femininity will depend on her philosophy and actions in her relations to man.

6

Loss of Identity as Woman and Wife

Every happy wife wants and expects to be identified as a wife. She wants to be respected and treated not only as a woman but, in addition, as a wife.

Most, if not all, women who are of age have been married, or are married, or hope to be married. Have you ever seen or heard of a woman who is capable of being married and who will admit that she has never married, has never hoped to be married, or never hopes to be married? Perhaps a few, but a very few!

Therefore, identity as a wife is an element which is essential to every marriage, to every family, and to the structure of our society. Identity as wife is included in all of these institutions.

A woman must first be accepted and identified as a woman before she can be socially accepted and identified as a wife to man. A man will not easily accept a woman for a wife who is not thought to be a real woman, a feminine woman, a woman who is wife material!

When man's attitude changes as to what a woman is and what she represents, then she will no longer exist as to what she was thought to be, though in fact she may have no physical change.

Things exist because they are believed to exist. An object exists in response to a mental image. The object will change every time when there's a change in the mental image.

So it is with a person. A person is whatever he or she is, because the person is perceived and believed to be so, though, in fact, there may be no facts to support the perception and belief. One may strongly see and strongly believe that another person is a crook, though there may not be a single fact to support such seeing and believing.

Perception and belief will control all conditions and facts, what they are, or what they appear to be. As perception and belief change, so do the conditions and facts perceived and believed to exist.

Of course, change becomes more readily apparent and acceptable when prompted by acts, words, or conduct. Thus it will be rather easy for man to change his perception and belief about what a woman and wife may be, when spurred on by her actions and philosophy of the Movement, with speed and strength added to the actions and philosophy, as well as to man's perception and belief about a woman, by the ERA if and when it becomes law.

Then, his image of her will change, just as one's image of a lighted room is changed by darkness.

With the change in man's image of a woman caused by the Movement, she, in reality, will be changed, being one person before the change in image, and another person after the change in image.

Before the change she was a woman, a person of feminine beauty, a person who perched on a pedestal in a women's world of unique respect and admiration afforded only to woman. After the change she is a person who competes with man, thinks like a man, talks like a man, and has all the demands of a man, appears and seems to be a man, and therefore is treated like a man!

She becomes a convenient part-time partner to man, furnishes him with sexual pleasures and other conveniences when needed by him. Her permanency with man, her protected status by man, and her interests once guarded by man will become man's temporary tools!

In short, she will no longer be thought to be the person considered to be woman before the change in man's image of her. Having been deprived of the image of being woman, treatment of her by man can no longer be the treatment customarily given to woman. The treatment given to her will be that of a convenient and part-time partner to man, with his having little if any responsibilities to her.

Part-time relations for the convenience of both may not be

so bad for a single woman, you think? Perhaps not, but, I believe that every woman wants the treatment and courtesy of man usually given to a woman, if the truth be known.

How about a wife in respect to such part-time treatment? Here we're talking about a woman living with a man in a permanent state of marriage. In such a state, no marriage can be enjoyable and happy unless both the husband and wife contribute to the mutual interests of the marriage. Treating a wife as a part-time convenient tool is not what she will likely tolerate, to any extent, anyway.

Certainly such relations would likely put an end to the marriage! Along with the marriage's ending will come problems for the wife, the husband, and the children of the marriage, as we shall see in following chapters.

Therefore, it is of much importance that a wife be treated like a woman, and more, because a wife expects more and needs more from a husband than does a single woman who may be sharing only part of her time with a man, neither one being morally, socially, or economically responsible to each other, unlike the case involving a husband and wife.

There's another point of interest, and it's this: Every happy wife or every woman who hopes to be a happy wife desires and expects to be identified as a wife. This is the role which she expects to be recognized by all.

Likely, no wife who is happily married would knowingly give up the identity as a wife.

What happens to the wife who adopts the strict philosophy of the Movement? She may do well to ponder her fate as a wife when she starts demanding that she be able to compete with her husband in life, demanding that she be free from her husband, free from her role as a mother, and free from all other traditional and customary roles as a wife. She may be wise to look at her road in life, where the road leads, and where it ends.

She may find that the road is filled with conflict and tension, with doubt and worry, with anxiety and fear, and with loneliness. As she travels the road, she may find that her marriage has become a house of neurosis and psychosis. She may long for peace and joy, but be unable to find it; she may search for belongingness and security, but find herself alone and afraid.

Yet, she has a choice before choosing to cut her ties as a wife and mother: She may go it alone in life, or she may choose to be forever happily married. It's her decision, her action, and her destiny to choose.

The proponents of the Movement say that a wife has been no more than a servant to her husband's wishes and demands, that she has been expected to submit sexually to him, expected to have children, and expected to take a back seat to her husband's wishes and demands. They say that a wife should change her status, let her personal desires and needs be separate from her husband and children, prevail over her marriage and her husband and her children.

The wife needs a new and different role in marriage, they say. However, they fail to define marriage. In fact, they have yet to recognize the possibility of a marriage even being able to exist if and when a wife takes on the new and different role proposed by the Movement, whatever the role may be, the role which they have not painted for us truly.

Nor do the proponents recognize that every woman's first and foremost personal desire and needs are, if the truth be known, to have a wonderful husband and lovely children. Nor do they tell us that a wife may never have a wonderful husband and lovely children if she chooses to place herself separate and apart from her husband and children in order to satisfy the expectations of the Movement.

They don't tell us that a wife may live forever happily married by making her husband and children a part of herself, by living in togetherness, yet at the same time living with freedom and individuality.

Also the proponents don't tell us that a happily married person is far more free than either a single or divorced person, as a general rule. The single or divorced person is preoccupied and frustrated with not having a congenial, compatible, and permanent mate. With such a state of mind, there can be very little real and lasting happiness. When unhappy or discontented, a person is never actually free. Mental chains, as a result of unhappiness, can be far worse than physical chains!

The Movement doesn't tell us that both man and woman have always been intended for each other, that there can never be supreme happiness living apart. Somewhere and somehow, a man and woman must learn to live together, if each expects to find happiness in life, and this is impossible by fighting each other with an anti-male or anti-female approach.

Whatever it is that has possessed woman to point a finger at man, who is supposedly responsible for the supposedly sorry plight of woman, is really not clear, let alone provable, if in fact there is anything at all!

The argument by the proponents of the Movement and ERA claim that women, especially wives, are chained to tradition and custom, such as accepting the husband's name upon marriage, and that a woman and wife is subservient to man and husband, living a certain life of bondage which has been carved and guarded and perpetuated by man.

The argument by the Movement goes on to say that a wife should not be subjected to sexual relations with her husband, should not be subjected to a state of pregnancy, and should not be subjected to being mistress of the home wherein the mistress is expected to care for young children, expected to cook and wash dishes, and make beds while the husband is at work in the office or in the field.

It is contended that somehow the husband has it much easier in such a marriage, that somehow the wife should change her role in such a regard, that somehow she should be able to do the job which her husband does, if she so desires, with sole discretion of the woman and wife to make the decision as to choice.

So, the wife who takes the advice of the Movement seeks a new status in marriage and in life. It's a status which is supposed to free the wife, give to her all means of finding fulfillment in marriage and in life.

Yet, a wife has always had a status in marriage which she has chosen. She has never been forced to live in a particular status.

She has lived her status in marriage and in society because she has wanted to do so, as a general rule. While the status has not been perfect, it has apparently been the best which we as imperfect human beings could provide.

The status has been far better than the new status proposed by the militant leaders of the Movement. They propose a status which attempts to force a place for the wife in a society which has always believed in a husband and wife living in a free and voluntary relationship, a relationship which can develop and grow free of forced rules of law. Remember, our system of government and society attempts to allow as much freedom as possible for its members, especially in the home where a husband and wife have always rejected control and invasion of privacy in the marriage and home.

Also, remember that, in our society here in the United States, our laws, including the proposed ERA, are no stronger than the will of the people, because our laws are supposed to be the will of the people, not the whim and caprice of a few militant persons who are unhappy and who attempt to force their unhappiness on the vast majority through unworkable and unjust laws.

No Congress, no legislature, and no court will be able to force the ERA upon the vast majority of husbands and wives in our society. You'll recall that Amendment Eighteen of the U.S. Constitution sought to prohibit the consumption of alcoholic beverages by the American people. However, since the amendment sought to force laws that did not represent the will of the people, it was repealed by Amendment Twenty-One to the Constitution.

The proposed ERA, if adopted to be Amendment Twenty-seven to the Constitution, will meet with quicker death than did the Prohibition Amendment. The latter amendment did not attempt to infringe on the relations between husband and wife and between parent and child, while the proposed ERA will, if passed, pose a constant threat to such relations.

So it is proposed that the members and followers of the Movement will find themselves, in the end, losing the very thing which they seek to recognize and preserve: identity and individuality for woman. Why is this so?

Because the individuality of woman will lose its identity and force through the act of competing with man. The followers of the Movement are in effect saying, "Let each of us be recognized as a person, as an individual," but their common cause is forced competition with man, which will lead to loss of image as women and to rejection by men, not men's recognition of a better and higher status and more respectibility for woman.

Here are some of the critical areas in which woman and wife will lose her individuality and respected status, should the ERA become law:

1. She will be subject to draft in the military service, the same as a man. Nor will she be entitled to special considerations once she is in the military, such as freedom from combat zones, freedom from hazardous duties and hardships.

2. She will not be entitled to preferential treatment in occupations because her physical strength is weaker than man's physical strength. The comforts afforded to her and not to man by an employer such as leave of absence for pregnancy, time off with her children, a minimum of night employment, lounges with sofas and refrigerators during work breaks, inside work during cold weather, and no "dirty work" will be stopped by the ERA, unless the same opportunities are afforded to man.

3. She will not be allowed to receive social security benefits not presently accorded man. For example, she presently is entitled to receive benefits at an earlier age than man and also receive benefits upon the death of her husband, although she may never have worked and contributed wages to social security. A man is not afforded the same benefits under the same circumstances.

4. She will not be eligible for retirement at an earlier age than man, though she presently has this benefit accorded by some employers. For example, some employers allow a woman to retire at the age of 60 or 62 years but allow men to retire only when reaching the age of 65.

5. Such jobs or occupations as airline stewardess, nursing, secretarial and others will not be exclusively the property rights

of woman. Man will be equally entitled to jobs or occupations which have traditionally been reserved only for woman.

6. Nor will woman receive preferential treatment in respect to the use and comforts of public utilities such as bathrooms and seating accommodations, though she is presently accorded preferential treatment.

7. A wife will become legally obligated for marital debts, including the husband's debts, which traditionally have been primarily imposed on the husband, including the wife's necessaries.

8. She will receive no preferential treatment in legal protection under laws primarily designed against assault, abuse, and vulgar treatment of woman.

9. She will receive no preferential treatment under laws designed to afford a woman the opportunity to do things at an earlier age than afforded a man, such as being eligible to marry at an earlier age than presently afforded man in some states.

10. She'll lose her right to alimony which she has enjoyed solely because she is a woman. Traditionally a woman has been entitled to seek alimony in divorce proceedings, and she has, in many cases, been entitled to it out of respect to special treatment for woman. Man has traditionally never been entitled to alimony. We'll have more on alimony in chapter 11 of this book.

11. Traditionally, a husband has been liable in most if not all states for a wife's legal fees and court costs in divorce proceedings. This liability cannot be imposed if the ERA becomes law.

12. Also a father has been traditionally liable for child support after a divorce or during separation between husband and wife. No longer can the courts expect to give preferential treatment to a mother in this respect, should the ERA become law. We'll have more on child support in chapter 12 of this book.

13. Courts have always granted custody of young children to the mother after legal divorce or during separation between the mother and father. Such preferential treatment will be unlawful should the ERA become law.

14. A woman cannot expect special treatment in receiving a prison sentence upon conviction for a crime. Judges have been

reluctant to send a mother to prison when she has had young children to care for, which opportunity has not been afforded a father.

These are, to mention only a few, distinctions between man and woman, husband and wife, which will be abolished by the ERA. In short, all legal, economic, and social distinctions between them will cease to exist. The special and protected status of woman will be in memory only. Her identity as a woman will be given very little public recognition, if any.

Last, but most important, is what man will think of woman should the ERA become a tool for venting woman's frustrations. While a woman who is identified with the Movement has already gained some disrespect from man based on my observations, rains and floods of his disrespect for her will surely come if and when the ERA becomes law and is daily waggled before his eyes in bitter and hostile disputes.

As true for man without the respect of woman, it's as true for woman that, without the respect of man, she can't have his love, his affection, and truly share happy companionship with him.

With the identity of femininity taken away from a wife, what will be the results in the relations between her and husband? If a wife wants to compete with man and act like a man, then she'll be treated like a man! Let's now turn to the issue of femininity.

7

Loss of Femininity

The beauty, the grace, the tenderness, the softness, the charm, the gentleness, the loveliness, the dignity, and the refined sensibility of a woman are femininity.

Without these things, there can be no femininity in woman. Take away these things, and femininity is gone. Once it is gone, a woman is powerless, not only with man, but in whatever position she finds herself. She then lives in a world stripped of recognition and distinction.

These things which make up femininity come from what woman thinks of herself, what others think of her, and how she appears both physically and mentally in her relation to others.

Femininity comes in the ways in which she talks, acts, walks, works, and reacts in life, in her relation to others. It is a philosophy, a culture, or a type of religion which woman has, respected and liked by man. It's a mark of distinction between her and man.

It's femininity which has charisma and power with man, and it's that which excites him about woman. Femininity is the primary key to the doors of success for her. Without it, she has little chance of equality, if any, with man.

Man's receptiveness to her, both the degree and kind of receptiveness, is conditioned and controlled by her femininity. What he thinks of her and what he does for her will depend on the nature of reception which she receives from him.

Man will act and react favorably to that which he respects and admires, and, without respect and admiration for woman, which is primarily based on femininity, he will receive from and give very little to her, nothing much of anything which he is not compelled to receive or give, whatever it may be.

As with a woman who believes and lives femininity, a man is very religious with his thoughts and desires about it. Just as femininity is bred by culture in a woman, so it is with man. With both it's a deep-rooted conviction, a conviction arising at the time of birth which is lived and practiced throughout life. With most people in our society, it's a way of life, just as wearing clothes, getting married, or going to school.

Femininity in woman is a Great Expectation which lives and lurks in every home, every school, every church, every job, every street and town, every organization, and in every corner of life in our society.

It is guarded and cherished by all. We inherited femininity, have cared for it, cultivated it and have liked it! It is part and parcel of our civilization. To recognize and respect the femininity of woman is to be civilized.

The femininity of woman stands out in life, as a soft rose does in a garden of thorns. In life, woman stands as a flower of femininity, giving radiance and fragrance to life.

Praise is song to her femininity, and joy of her femininity is refreshing to life, and femininity is the link which has been most distinguished in keeping man and woman together. It's the peculiar quality belonging only to woman, but honored and protected and loved and respected by man.

It's an eternal flame which has lighted the path of life for woman, travelled with her, carrying man as a willing shield and companion as she goes.

Femininity is perpetually planted and perpetually cultivated and perpetually harvested. It has spawned and breathed life for both woman and man, and it has given to woman the mighty and respected place in life which is shared and enjoyed by man.

It's a life which is built, kept, and comforted by philosophy and actions of both man and woman, but adversely to change the philosophy and actions of either woman or man or both, and the life of femininity will also be adversely changed.

Understanding, patience, and working together with love will allow both man and woman to grow in equality. With these things they can grow and work together as equal partners. By working with such qualities, each will voluntarily share mutual respect.

Voluntary and mutual change in their relations for the purpose of further understanding between them is not only desirable but necessary if they are to grow and mature in their relations in order that each may fully appreciate and fulfill objectives in life, whatever they may be.

Since man and woman live together in society, they must learn to enjoy and be happy in their relations. No one will, I believe, propose that man or woman can be happy without sharing their lives, whether in marriage, in an occupation, or whatever.

It does, therefore, follow that a positive and healthy attitude must exist between them. Whatever is done or said to change such an attitude will result in poor relations, injurious to both.

The attitude of the Movement is too much competing with man, too demanding of him, which has an air of being anti-male. The attitude carries with it antagonism and resentment toward man. The reported saying of Mrs. Imelda Marcos, wife of President Ferdinand E. Marcos of the Philippines, in her address to the International Women's Year conference held in Mexico City, Mexico, in June of 1975, is that the Movement ". . . has become too competitive, demanding and anti-male."[4] She is reported to have further said of the philosophy and actions of the Movement in her address at the conference that:

> The demand for equality has too often had overtones of revenge, the venting of grievances, the acquisition of advantage, the aggression of concealed hatred and envy. . . .[5]

Such demands, which carry envy and hatred and ultimatums for immediate action, filled with frustration of woman, with no known origin and with no known objectives or goals, other than to vent such frustration on man, will do nothing for woman and

[4]The *Mobile Register,* June 21, 1975, p. 2-A.
[5]*Ibid.*

the image of femininity except destroy them and, therefore, result in the loss of her desirable relation to man. Her recognition
and hope for equality with man will receive a harmful blow by
such loss.

Remember, resentment between man and woman, which is
being fostered by the Movement (though perhaps in good faith
by many of its followers), is destructive to good relations between man and woman and will become even more destructive
by legal actions and threats to be fostered by the ERA, if it
becomes law.

The results of resentment, demands, competition, envy, and
hatred will be losses to the image of woman, social, economic and
political, as well as loss to the image of femininity, the exact
opposite of gains for woman hoped for by the Movement. Such
losses will be increased by the ERA, should it become law,
since the ERA will increase and sanction the effects of philosophy
and actions of the Movement.

While the loss of social and economic identity for a woman
will greatly dwarf and diminish her respect and status as a
woman, loss of her femininity reduces her image as a woman to
a blurring shadow of the giant image which she has had and
still deserves.

Without love and respect for femininity, a woman is nothing
more than a tool to be used and discarded by man at his convenience. She'll be used for whatever purpose she may serve man,
with no strings attached! This is true, because man very seldom
takes care of that for which he has no respect.

This is the road on which a woman may find herself, should
she follow the Movement and therefore compete with man. In
such a role she'll be treated and respected with conduct becoming a man. Such treatment will be in harmony with the philosophy and actions of the Movement, to gain momentum with the
ERA, should it become law.

With loss of a woman's identity as a woman and wife and
loss of identity in femininity, what else is to be expected? How
about the flowers on the wedding anniversary? Only a woman's
feminine love and charm are deserving. Let a wife open her

doors and place her chair. These things are done by man only for feminine beauty, love, and respect.

If a wife chooses to abandon her role as a wife and mother, then let her pay her way through life. Only the wife who loves and conducts herself in a feminine role will be economically protected.

Let her repair the washing machine and dishwasher and change her auto tires, for these are roles awarded by the philosophy and actions of the Movement and the proposed ERA. These roles are fitting and proper in the new status sought by the Movement. For sure, these roles will be the end products of the Movement, refined and polished by the ERA, should it become law.

Since a woman who chooses the new status will not receive protection from the abuse and vulgarity from which she has traditionally been protected, then let her fight her own battles against maltreatment and uncouthness.

Grime and filth in human relations will be hers with which to contend, without help from man.

In times of need, the husband won't be around to lend his broad shoulders as a cushion for his wife's distresses. The wife who chooses to identify with the Movement and, therefore, against man can't expect to be included in her husband's social life. There are too many other women who care for and seek such a life with him!

Let her go her way, and let him go his. Let both ignore their marriage vows. Why should they love, protect, and care for each until death do they part?

With loss of identity as a woman and loss of femininity as a woman, where's the link with which they are to be held together, as husband and wife? Togetherness will be mutilated by the Movement and buried by the ERA should it become law!

Man and others in society have revered and protected the image of femininity, just as they have the image of the American flag or the Bible, but likely with more reverence and respect for femininity than for these things.

My observations have been that the Movement hopes to do

away with the image of femininity as one of the best moves which will help to destroy the distinctions between man and woman.

For example, Elizabeth Reid, an Australian delegate to the International Women's Year conference, which we've spoken of already, is reported to have said:

> . . . Women must realize the reality of the sexism which hurts them.[6]

Of course sexism is part of the image of femininity, with no need for anything in such image but beauty and respect. Certainly femininity is not an evil and destructive force which is expected to come in the stealth of the night with intent and determination to destroy woman!

Yet, the Movement subtly seeks to brainwash woman so that she may see femininity or sexism as a symbol of evilness to woman's plight in life.

The Australian delegate was reported to further have stated in respect to the danger in woman's sexism and in doing away with the image of sexism, that what is required is:

> . . . as much a revolution in the heads of people as it does the modification of the structures which reinforce these destructive values.[7]

In other words, I take this statement to mean that the respect and value placed on the image of femininity or sexism of woman must not let the image held for femininity or sexism stand in the way of the revolutionary changes in society waged in the crusade by the Movement.

Thus the image of femininity, as being an obstacle to the success of the revolutionary changes staged by the Movement, must be removed. Therefore, the best and perhaps only way to

---

[6]Op. cit., the *Mobile Register.*
[7]Op. cit., the *Mobile Register.*

remove it is to change the thinking of woman so that she has no respect for her femininity or sexism, and that she will, once the image is removed, think and conduct herself in such a way so that not only woman but man will abhor instead of cherish the image of femininity, paving the way to clearly and completely obliterate the distinctions between man and woman.

The Movement is, therefore, staging a crusade which is not femininistic or pro-woman but is anti-femininistic and anti-woman. Such crusade can't be said to be in the interests of woman, for what is anti-woman will not enhance or increase her equality of rights under the ERA which will also be anti-woman but will lessen or take away rights which already exist for her. You can't do something against a person's interests and say that by doing so you're building and protecting his or her interests!

First, what woman doesn't like favorable masculine attention? All mature and well-adjusted women do. But, such attention will be short-lived if the ERA is ratified, taking away the image of femininity which is the thing which attracts such attention.

Secondly, what would woman's world be without the reverence and respect for woman's image of femininity? I'm not only talking about indulgence in sexual pleasures, but what would be woman's bargaining power, not only in the economic areas of life but in all relations to man and others in society, without the image of femininity?

As a woman, what would be your chances for success with your husband, with a prospective husband, with a prospective employer, with employees, or with anyone else without a good image of femininity? Without a feminine touch and a feminine appearance, you as a woman would not be too desirable with these persons in any kind of relationship with them! So, as a woman, you should think long and hard before thinking and doing that which would result in loss of femininity.

8

Man's Counterattacks

While women of the Movement make demands for competition with man, brew and serve resentment and antagonism to him, sprinkled with envy and hatred, and issue ultimatums out of frustration for change, will man idly stand by with meekness and obedience?

Not likely! It's not man's nature to be captured and live by a philosophy and actions such as practiced by the Movement, the things which will turn meekness and obedience into aggression and independence. Nor will he be bound by the results of the ERA if it becomes law.

The American man has always believed in freedom, especially in his relationship to woman, and he will vigorously oppose any restraints on such freedom. Therefore, the woman who expects to force a change in his relations to her, an adverse change to his happiness, can expect blistering counterattacks from him!

Man will not study and learn the lesson now being taught by the Movement, a lesson which seeks to force relations between man and woman. Without acceptance of such lesson, its subject matter will not be applied to him. Demands and ultimatums from woman will be sent back to her with messages which will cause her to retreat and to give up victories once won for the image of woman.

The pedestal on which she once perched will be yanked away, and her image of femininity shall grow dim. By her acceptance and practice of the philosophy and actions advocated by the Movement, equality of rights for her will receive a drastic setback, because recognition of equality of rights cannot survive in an atmosphere where woman and man are fighting and opposing each other in areas which should represent common causes, areas such as marriage, parent and child relations, sex life, the school, the church, and mutual rights and duties in the home.

Man's counterattacks to such philosophy and actions will render blows of defeat to her. The glory which she has enjoyed as a woman will melt and seep into obscurity.

The revolutionary changes sought by her will be met with revolutionary resistance from man! There'll be attacks and counterattacks. Her rights, once recognized and cherished by man, will become casualties.

Yesterday's recognition by him of her image as a person of feminine beauty will go unnoticed. The protection of her world, the special courtesies afforded to her and the influence once held by her in relation to man will go unattended, and, without the attention needed for the life of these things, they will weaken and perish.

Instead of seeking to further mutual understanding and acceptance between man and woman, the Movement breeds and perpetuates an air of distrust and rejection in their relations by making demands for competition, by issuing ultimatums for immediate action, by giving vibes of envy and vengeance, and by demanding special advantages for women, all supposedly because man has long kept woman in a world of both oppression and suppression, a philosophy which is characteristic of that of the militancy of minority groups and student revolutionists of the 1960s.

Woman can't expect to gain favorable recognition by such principles, principles levelled at man with pricks of resentment and antagonism. By doing so she will receive his counterattacks of forceful revenge and suppression, indifference and apathy. He will attempt to crush woman's acts for revolutionary changes, not only crush such acts but give punishment to her by crushing her world of femininity through indifference.

The chivalry, the protection, and the gentleness held for woman will be exchanged for "survival of the fittest"!

Woman will be ignored and rejected, left to fend for herself, with no remedy unless she returns to her world, where both she and man have had mutual understanding, mutual love, mutual respect, mutual happiness, and where they have also had changes in growth of their relations in order to improve their existence together in a world made for both.

The philosophy and actions of the Movement are, in effect, attacks on voluntary, happy, and workable relations between man and woman, where attacks will have the effects of hurting relations in marriage, hurting relations between parent and child, hurting relations between employer and employee, hurting relations in schools, in churches and in other areas of human relations, and such attacks will be met by man's strength of resistance, not only defensively but offensively.

Not only will man defend his position of voluntary, happy, and workable relations with others, but he will use whatever means are necessary to drive out the forces which attempt to attack his position!

The demands, ultimatums, envy, hatred, and resentment spread by the Movement, hopefully to be codified and enforced by the ERA, will adversely affect relations between man and woman, because such philosophy and actions are resented by human nature. It's only natural for man to retaliate to that which seeks to make him unhappy!

Let's take a wife, for example, who chooses to adopt and practice the philosophy and actions of the Movement and see their adverse effects on her life and marriage.

A marriage is a bed of expectations! Both the husband and wife expect certain things and certain conduct from each other. Adjustment to changes is not always readily acceptable, especially if the changes are not in line with the expectations. A change in a marital relationship may be received with approval, or it may be met with some resistance or met with vigorous and stern resistance.

The change may not only be met with stern resistance but may be met with lashing counterattacks! A wife who voluntarily chooses to lose both her identity as wife and femininity will very likely feel, soon or late, the sting of such counterattacks in multiplying numbers.

First of all, most husbands will not accept the new status proposed by the Movement. For example, a husband will continue to expect the wife to be mistress of the home, primarily responsible for cooking, or seeing that it's done; primarily responsible for the care of the children while he's at work, or seeing that it's done; to first be mother and wife before an equal rightist (and the two roles will not always go together); to first share the problems and responsibilities for maintaining an efficient and happy home before sharing the philosophy and actions of the equal rightists. (And these two roles will not always go together because the philosophy and actions of the equal rightists, as pronounced by the leaders of the Movement say, "Leave me alone; I'll do what I want to do. Although I'm legally married, I may never choose to be a mother or wife because these positions may not make me equal to my husband. I'll show him that I can do anything that he does.")

Better yet, the Movement has a cohesive force against being identified with man. It seeks militant independence and aloofness from man instead of individuality for a woman. Instead of understanding that individuality and togetherness, for man and woman can and do go together in successful and happy marriages, the Movement seems only to understand, advocate, and identify woman under the label of equal rights, which will, however, as preached by the Movement, lead to a cold and calculated separation between man and woman, since man and woman don't grow together by fighting each other!

Secondly, a husband's expectations of his wife are not consistent with the philosophy and actions of the Movement. He enjoys her status as a beautiful and feminine woman, while the Movement and proposed ERA will cause her to lose this status and cause her to attempt to compete with a husband in a man's world. The husband will not accept such a role by the wife. Therefore, the more that she competes in a man's world, the more that he will counterattack her actions and philosophy in the new status proposed by the Movement.

When she attempts to show him that she need not sexually submit to him, he'll find a woman who will; when she refuses to bear children, he'll find a woman who will; when she refuses to be mistress of the home, he'll find a woman who will; when she insists on putting a working career before being a wife and mother, he'll rebel. By doing these things she'll have lost his respect. And a husband doesn't care to live with a wife who takes away his respect.

Loss of her identity in femininity and as a wife will chill his feelings for her, turning his warmth for her into a windy chilliness.

In addition to the counterattacks already mentioned, the husband may be expected to follow several courses of conduct. First, he may ignore the wife's attempts to seek the new role; secondly, he may attempt to reason with her in order to convince her that the new role is not healthy for the marriage; thirdly, he may go his way and let her go hers; fourthly, he may choose to abandon her. As you can see, none of these solutions is good for a husband and wife who want to be forever happily married because they'll only lead to separation and divorce.

So the very recognition and personal identity which the Movement seeks for woman will be destroyed by the Movement's own philosophy and actions! The unhappiness of the few militant leaders of the Movement will be imposed, in some cases, on other women who are caught up in the Movement and swept, tossed, and crushed by its harsh winds of Frustration and Anxiety.

Unhappiness will beget unhappiness. Onward! Onward! Unhappiness will march. Understanding between husband and wife will be slaughtered in its sweeping path. Its swathing blows will run head on into the husband's sharpened and stinging counterattacks!

His scythe will mow with awesome force. As the path of unhappiness is deepened and widened where husband and wife tread, understanding and growth between them will smolder in ruination. Peaceful living for them will become a world of frustration. Mental Disorder will become Ruler.

9

Mental Disorder

A happy wife enjoys and dreams of always receiving a warm and passionate reception from her husband, and, if happy, he is always looking forward to greeting her with a warm embrace. They meet and share with a feeling of trust, a feeling of calmness, a feeling of being partners for a lifetime, a feeling that neither one will intentionally cause problems for their marriage.

With mutual trust and understanding, nothing in life for them becomes too great to overcome. They may have temporary setbacks and perhaps disagreements between them, but never intentional creation of problems directed toward tearing their marriage apart.

Each has his and her individual world, but always these two worlds from a world of unity for their marriage. Each one will build upon his or her individuality which remains distinctive, but their individualities will always contribute to the love and understanding which unite them.

Neither one will say or do anything which will be intended to injure the other. Praise by each and for each will be a common standard in the marriage, and failures will be shared and mutually solved, keeping in mind that unhappiness for one will mean unhappiness for the other, and that success for one will mean success for both, because whatever affects one in the unity of their relations will also affect the other.

Nor will either one attempt to envy the other, because envy only creates resentment, bringing ill will into their marital relations, and, in an atmosphere of ill will, neither one can enjoy the mutual pleasures of their relationship.

Both know that envy and resentment bring about destructive competition between them, unlike positive results that come from working in a spirit of cooperation brought about by mutual help and mutual understanding which will produce harmonious growth for them.

The husband and wife both know that each has a far greater chance of success and happiness when living in a setting of kindness and good will rather than when living in discord and antagonism.

They know that a positive relationship between them will produce positive results for their well-being, unlike a negative relationship which will produce failure.

Too, they know that a spirit of straightforwardness, a spirit of mutual respect, and a spirit of tolerance for shortcomings will set the stage for a deep and sincere and pleasant and lasting relationship, and that such relationship will lend itself to freedom for growth in meaningful and good things in life.

Such relationship will create an awareness not only of the needs of each but the needs for a happy and lasting life together. The strength, the weakness, and the needs for improvement in such a relationship can be faced with an open and calm mind, with a willingness by each to do whatever is necessary in order to generate and keep happiness.

Today, each will work together for a happy tomorrow. Each will let go of past mistakes and think and do that which will lend to happiness for the present, letting the happiness for the present build and multiply for the needs of tomorrow.

Both will understand that success or failure will be determined and controlled by a state of mind, a state of mind based on hope and faith for each other or a state of mind based on envy and fear for each other's station in life. Fruits of their relationship will be determined by the kind of mental seed and mental cultivation devoted to the relationship.

They know that likeness begets likeness. Trust attracts trust, while distrust attracts distrust; envy and resentment will attract the same, while good will generates a spirit of cooperation, a spirit of understanding and tolerance.

A smile given will receive a smile in return, while scorn begets scorn. Insults, degradation, and unreasonable demands made in an attack on one will cause and bring about retaliation from the other. Also known is that an attack by one is likely to be met by a nasty counterattack from the other.

True, for a single woman who hopes to have a pleasant relationship with a single man as well as for husband and wife, is the principle which holds that a happy mind functions much better than one which is unhappy, and a happy mind creates happy results, unlike the unhappy mind which creates frustration and confusion.

Harmony in relations between man and woman is created and maintained when they're at peace with each other. Without peace they can't coexist in a tranquil state. When at war with each other, nothing goes right! This is especially true for a husband and wife who have chosen to live together in a permanent state. In this state, the attitude of each should be cooperative, understanding, and in a live-and-let-live world in order to peacefully exist together, always free of degradation, insult, envy, hatred, fear, agitation, and intolerance.

Instead of grooming man and woman to live in a state of peace, the Movement has groomed them to live in a state of war by making unreasonable demands on man, by blaming him for woman's unhappiness, by being envious of man, by issuing frustrated ultimatums to man with no known purpose in mind, by seeking special gains for woman based solely on sex, by demanding that woman be allowed to compete with man at her own whim and caprice, and by attempting to set woman against man and man against woman.

The Movement hopes to change the whole structure of society for both woman and man, against the will and cooperation of a vast majority of both women and men, a move which can hardly avoid a clashing war between man and woman. In such a state of turmoil stands a fence of resentment and agitation between man and woman, the fence growing higher and wider, a fence built on mental disorder and not on reason and experience.

For man and woman to live with resentment and agitation directed at each other is to create a state of anxiety, and anxiety will beget anxiety, until the desire and enthusiasm for peacefully living together vanish.

Such sorry conditions will result in a state of war between man and woman, to be continued with the adoption and ratification of the ERA.

The mental war started and perpetrated by the Movement will rage on and on unless reason is allowed to prevail over emotions. While the mental war rages, man and woman can expect to experience painful relations, capped with mental anguish.

Bickering, nagging, belittling, verbal attacking, and verbal counterattacking between husband and wife brought on by the philosophy and actions of the Movement, to be refueled by the proposed ERA, will build mountains of mental problems for marriage.

Relations between husband and wife will be governed and controlled by stress. Life will be clothed in mental disorder!

For some, feelings and actions between them will become as taut as fiddle strings, cold as steel, impersonal as stone, and unwelcoming as a deadly disease. The existence and survival of a happy marriage under such conditions have no better chance than a snowflake when dropped into a foaming volcano with acres of burning lava!

At first, tempers will flare, and then accusations against each will become vicious and cutting. Weaknesses of each will be held up and dangled at each other by attacks and counterattacks. Ridicule will become the order of each day.

Then the rains of dissension will pour. Large drops of threats, cruelty, hostility, resentment, frustration, greed, selfishness, sadness, sorrow, infidelity, name-calling, loss of respect, loneliness, and rejection will blanket the marriage. Emotional tension will woo and swoon the marriage, penetrating with poison its very existence.

Stability of the marriage will collapse. Interest in it will cease to exist. Every vein of hope for the marriage will vanish. Avenues for relief will run into a one-way street; divorce court!

With all the psychological problems looming over the marriage like flashing and thundering clouds carrying news of a dreadful storm, husband and wife will become engulfed in a web of hysteria. Emotions will prevail over reason; understanding will give way to impatience; frustration will win over calmness; joy of being together will be replaced by a yearning to be apart.

So the endurance of the marriage will meet with agony, and the thin line between love and hate will disappear. Hate being allowed to exist, love will take wings and fly from the marriage.

Ugliness and wickedness will stage performances for the marriage, drinking and talking the dregs and waste of man and woman, a forlorn husband and wife carrying a tiresome load of tiresome burdens.

During the process of breakdown in the marriage, there will be burdens of conflict and estrangement between husband and wife. Emotional tension caused by differences will chew and tear at the marriage, with the marriage being ground into bits.

The feeling of estrangement will alienate love and affection. A feeling of separation will stampede and wipe out the feeling of hope for togtherness. There'll be a feeling of withdrawal and development of separate worlds, one for husband and one for wife.

The feeling of trust, of forgiveness, of having individuality in a successful marriage, of being able to communicate, and of being forever happily married will disappear. Instead, there'll be thoughts of irritation, frustration, and worry which will become as common as the air one breathes.

Again, we may say that the Movement and proposed ERA will destroy the very things which the Movement advocates: recognition and equality for woman. When her status and recognition in relation to man are badly damaged, by whom is she to be recognized? No one, unless by man, since it's not recognition from woman which the proponents are seeking.

To whom is the woman to be equal? No one, unless to man. Once a good relationship with man is destroyed, there'll be no one else with whom to compare and measure equal rights for woman!

Such will be the case for the woman who is maladjusted to man. It'll be her case if she seeks to blame man for her own unhappiness and for her own low image of herself. Proper image and happiness won't come until such a woman has a good self-image, and such an image won't come by blaming man. Competition with man, whether by legal battle through the proposed ERA or otherwise, will not give self-assurance and security in life to the woman. The answer lies in her state of mind.

She must first consider herself as a worthwhile individual and conduct herself as such. Then she'll be recognized as she sees herself, a worthy person. In a discussion with my wife, Gladys, in respect to this point she told me that, "I know that I am a person in my own right with my own personality and that I can cope with life; therefore, I do not have to prove to myself that I am an individual. This feeling or image of myself permits me to identify with my husband and fill the role of wife joyfully and freely, with no reservations, no inhibitions, and no feeling of inferiority."

Does the woman who thinks that she must compete with man and be recognized by him in the name of equal rights feel insecure and inferior? A mature and well-adjusted woman doesn't have to prove to herself that she's equal to man by competing with him.

Nor does she have to have a law on the books so stating. The image which she has of herself is likely the image which others have of her. Others will accept her for what she accepts and feels about herself.

Mental disorders will not add to her self-image, but, to the contrary, will lower such an image. A state of confusion will only hamper perception and growth for a healthy image.

Along with mental disorder caused by the philosophy and actions of the Movement and proposed ERA, there's another form of insecurity which will be an offshoot of troubled relations with man: sexual inadequacy for the woman. In an attempt to align herself with other women when feeling rejected by man, to whom will she turn for sexual relations? Out of fear, out of rejection, out of a feeling of unbelongingness, and out of loneliness, will the woman turn to homosexuality in order to relieve a sense of desperation? Let's discuss this point in the next chapter.

10

Homosexuality

Sexual relations between a man and a woman are considered to be normal in our society, especially in marriage, which is seen as a family setting.

The acceptance by society of sexual relations in marriage serves at least two basic functions: first, it allows both the man and the woman to satisfy sexual drives and, second, it perpetuates society by birth of new members for society, without the social stigma attached to sexual relations between man and woman outside the marriage or the family setting.

But society has yet to approve, to any noticeable degree, sexual relations between two persons of the same sex, sexual relations between two females or sexual relations between two males. Such relations are referred to as homosexuality.

Homosexuality is pretty much condemned by society, although recently society has shown a little, but very little tolerance toward it. It is classified as deviant behavior, meaning that it is not the normal and acceptable way to engage in sexual relations.

It may be argued that homosexuality does cut down on the rate of births since the only way which society knows and accepts for bringing about the birth of a human being is through sexual relations between man and woman, not taking into consideration the process of artificial insemination.

Also, it may be argued that a majority of men and women who are married as husbands or wives and those men and women who hope to be married do not approve of being married to a homosexual.

Therefore, based on these assumptions, homosexuality does have a material bearing on marital relations and on an acceptable perpetuation of the human race in our society. In addition, some have moral and religious convictions which are not consistent with the acceptance of homosexuality.

How does homosexuality fit into the scheme of the philosophy and the actions of the Movement as well as into the consequences of the ERA?

The philosophy consists of a crusade which is, on the visible surface, a crusade for the rights of women, but the philosophy is, in effect, a projection of resentment, hostility, antagonism, and rejection in the relations between women and men.

Actions of the Movement consist of demands on men for competition by women in men's occupation, in business, in politics, and in other areas, as well as demands for changes in marriage relations—such as the wife being allowed to choose between pursuing a career outside the home or pursuing a role as mistress of the home; demands for changes in positions for women in religious and civic organizations, as well as changes in positions involving professions and schools; demands for changes in laws governing such areas as abortion, alimony, child support; and other demands for changes which will eradicate all distinctions between women and men in the political and the social and the economic worlds.

The philosophy and actions of the Movement each feed on and multiplies from the other: the more that demands are made, the more that the philosophy is spread; the more that the philosophy is spread, the more that the demands increase, both the philosophy and actions hopefully to be sanctioned and enforced through the ERA, if it becomes law.

These conditions will result in estranged relations between men and women. Such relations will result in homosexuality for some. Why is this so? Out of sheer desperation! A desperation to seek and fulfill a need for belongness, an acceptance by others, approval of self, a cure for loneliness, and also to fulfill the need for sexual adequacy.

Therefore, a woman may wish to contemplate and analyze her future sexual relations which may be affected by the Movement and the consequences of the ERA if it becomes law.

She may be faced with estranged relations which will result

in her being isolated from men, and living in an atmosphere of isolation is not conducive to building and maintaining sexual relations with the opposite sex.

Too, with resentment and antagonism existing between a woman and a man they can't be expected to care for sexual relations with each other, and a passive or even resentful attitude toward sexual relations between a woman and a man will likely end with no sexual relations at all!

Also, negative relations between a woman and a man will create an air of distrust, and neither woman nor man really cares for mutual sexual relations when they distrust each other. This is especially true when distrust exists between a husband and wife.

And without a man around to care for her, a woman is likely to become lonely, and loneliness is a dreadful and an unbearable feeling.

With loneliness, with isolation from man, with distrust for man, with resentment and antagonism from man, and with the need for self-fulfillment, the woman will turn to those who will accept her and to those who will become substitutes for man, and such persons may likely be, and will be in many cases, those of her own sex, other women.

In the homogenous group of her own sex, the woman will encounter social structures which provide conditions, learning patterns, and justifications favorable to the occurrence of homosexual contacts.

Because of the needs for acceptance, for belongness, and for sexual adequacy the woman will become vulnerable to the social structures within the group. In the group will be some homosexuality, because some women, like some men, will engage in homosexuality if there's no other outlet for sexual drive.

Homosexual behavior will emerge, not only from the need to fulfill sexual drive but also as a result of adapting to the forces and pressures within the social structures of the group.

At least some women are not likely to fight or reject, for long, the pressures and rationale of the group which makes homosexuality a way of life. Soon a woman will become obedient to such pressures, willingly or not, rather than be rejected by the group, the only place where she may find acceptance after being rejected by man or after she rejects man.

Likely, the woman will find it less painful to accept the norms of the group rather than go through life without sexual engagement and also without approval from others.

Having turned to others of her own sex, she will be enticed by and internalize the acceptable norms of homosexuals in her group. In a group of her own sex the woman is placed in a psychosexual atmosphere or setting which is conducive to homosexuality. In this group she can identify and be accepted by the group.

Having been ridiculed and rejected by man and possibly deserted by him, she finds a home of acceptance in the homosexual group. Here she may find sexual adequacy, which she was unable to find with man. Then she can feel justified in her refusal or failure to adequately fulfill the role of sexual relations with man.

Once in the homogenous group, the woman can avoid the hostility and failure in her relations with man. Once in the group and having adapted to the group norms, she may find that homosexuality is a way of championing the cause of identifying with woman rather than identifying with man.

Such identity may, however, mean more isolation from man than existed before becoming amenable to the norms of the homogenous group. Thus in this event her behavior is likely to become reinforced by anti-male philosophy which is, in effect, being preached by the Movement.

How about man? He may very well turn to homosexuality as a result of estrangement from woman and as a result of dissatisfaction with her. Like the woman, he also needs a feeling of sexual adequacy, a feeling of being able to identify with others and to be accepted by them.

Having been rejected by woman and being dissatisfied with her, he too may find satisfaction in being with a homogenous group of men. Being a homosexual, for him, may be far better than living in sexual frustration with a woman. He, too, can rationalize homosexuality so that it is acceptable, when he has a feeling of rejection by woman and a feeling of sexual inadequacy.

Neither all women nor all men who are misfits within a normal man-woman sexual relationship will become homosexual. Some will, however. Generally, neither man nor woman will forever live without some attempts at sometimes finding some way by which to receive sexual fulfillment.

Hence, assuming that the philosophy and actions of the Movement result in homosexuality for some persons, it may be further assumed that passage of the ERA would add to homosexuality by further isolating some women from some men.

Therefore, adoption and ratification of the ERA as law will have a negative effect on marriage, family, and also on the heterogeneous social structure of our society by promoting homosexuality.

11

Alimony

Very likely a vast majority of our society is against broken homes for children, against disintegration of the family as an institution, against an increase in the divorce rate, and against a needy wife having to fend helplessly for herself in order to seek mere survival.

Yet, the Movement and proponents of the ERA are, in effect, asking for these very things, because under laws of the ERA we can expect the issue of alimony to contribute to these things in life. However, before going into these matters let's define alimony.

What is alimony? It is an allowance awarded to one party (usually the wife), paid or given by another party (usually the husband), as required by court order, when either a legal separation or a divorce is granted by the court.

Alimony may be a sum in money or a sum in property or part of both. It may be an award in lump sum or in periodic payments, usually weekly or monthly. Alimony can be awarded for a particular duration or for an indefinite period, depending on the court order.

In awarding a sum for alimony, the court considers the customary living standards of the party (usually the wife) who is to receive it, as well as her actual needs and her financial ability, including her ability to earn a living, and also, the financial ability and needs of the party (usually the husband) who is required to pay alimony are considered in arriving at a sum to be paid.

When a husband or wife seeks a legal divorce, each is highly concerned with financial rights and obligations that each will have after the court grants the divorce. For example, a husband is concerned with how much alimony he may be required to pay to his wife, should a divorce be granted, and this has especially been true prior to some recent court decisions which have not always required a husband to pay alimony to an ex-wife.

On the other hand, a wife is concerned with how much alimony, if any, she may be granted, should there be a divorce. The husband and wife each know that it takes more money to maintain a separate home for each than it does when both are living in the same home.

Therefore, the probability of receiving alimony is a very significant and influential factor in helping a husband or wife to decide whether or not one or both should press for a divorce. For good or bad, oftentimes a husband is reluctant to seek a divorce if he is advised that he may be required to pay alimony to his wife, should a divorce be granted, especially if the expected sum of alimony is predicted to be rather high. Oftentimes he will seek reconciliation of his marriage, rather than run the risk of having to pay alimony should a divorce be granted.

Many times I've had husbands tell me during counseling in respect to seeking a divorce that, "If I didn't have to pay alimony, I'd get a divorce today!" So, in light of the probability of having to pay alimony, especially if predicted to be high, some husbands have gone back home, reconciled differences with their wives, and learned to live happily married.

Therefore, the probability of having to pay alimony has, many times, for many husbands, caused them to back off from seeking a divorce. Such restraint has allowed good sense and sound judgment to prevail over hasty, flaring, and groundless emotions. Consequently, many marriages have been saved in this manner, and many of the marriages have turned out to be for a lifetime, happy at that!

Also, a wife will, many times, back off from a divorce should the probability exist that she may receive no alimony or only a small sum of alimony, should a divorce be sought. I've heard many wives state something like this: "For what he's done to me, I think that I should receive at least one-half of what he makes. I can't live on any less!" When advised that the court would not likely grant nearly as much as she expected, she has disappointingly resounded with, "There's no way that I'll settle for anything less!"

So she has gone back home, reconciled differences with her husband, and learned to live happily married. The restraining effect of the probability of not receiving the expected sum of alimony has also caused her to allow common sense to prevail over emotions.

Some of the leaders of the Movement reluctantly admit that the ERA will have an adverse effect on mothers and wives who contemplate receiving alimony, and that a wife and a husband will each be treated at arms-length by the courts, with little or no concern for the real needs of a mother and wife, simply because the courts will be faced with the so-called law of equal rights. Special consideration for special and genuine problems will have to yield to the intent of bad law! The intent of the ERA will be to treat the husband and wife at arms-length.

Therefore, a wife and mother will no longer receive alimony simply and only because she is a wife or mother, regardless of her desperate needs, once the ERA becomes law, if it does. Under such law the needs of the husband are just as important and will receive just as favorable treatment as will the needs of the wife. To rule otherwise would be for the courts to discriminate against husbands, flying in the teeth of the very law (ERA) that is intended to do away with discrimination against husbands in respect to alimony in divorce proceedings.

Alimony can't be based on sex! Such consideration is totally new to the concept of common law, the legal tradition and customs inherited from the mother country, England, which holds that a husband is not entitled to alimony under any circumstances.

With common law, only a wife is entitled to alimony. Her right to alimony with common law has been a right arising solely from the status of being married. Her needs, her wealth, or lack of wealth, or the husband's needs, or wealth, or lack of it have nothing to do with a wife's right to alimony in common law. About the only thing that could bar her right to alimony at common law was proof of adultery against her in divorce proceeding.

State legislatures and courts have not, however, waited for the ERA to become law before doing away with rights of a wife to receive alimony as a pure matter of legal right, solely because she may have been a mother and a wife. As woman has demanded release from chores in the home which were traditionally assumed to be her chores, demanded rights to work in offices and factories, demanded rights to come and go without the normal restraints placed on her by custom and tradition, and demanded that a husband no longer be treated by the law as head of household, the state legislatures and the courts have not received the demands with deaf ears.

Many of the state legislatures have now passed laws which make a husband as well as a wife eligible for alimony. Courts now carefully consider a wife's request for alimony. In Florida, for example (which state has no-fault divorce), a wife is more apt not to receive alimony than to receive it. Thus the demands by women for changes in life are coupled to additional responsibilities for them. Hence, their demands have resulted in additional duties, duties to support themselves and their minor children, and not in more rights!

So, as the Movement has rocketed with demands and pressures for freedom from the restraints of man, child, and marriage, women find themselves with imposition of new and additional duties, some which will not be too pleasant. For example, how about the wife who has been loyal, devoted, and who has worked hard with her husband in building a home and rearing the children for twenty years, but is suddenly bumped by the husband for a new twenty-year-old wife? The ex-wife now has no trade with which to make a living and no emotional or financial security. In case her ex-husband is able to do so, should he be required to pay alimony? Perhaps so. However, the present trend is that she will find herself having to make a living without a trade, without emotional and financial security, and without alimony!

The mother and wife will be the loser of alimony which is barred more and more by demands made by the Movement for so-called equal rights, more so than will the father and husband. When very young, children need the care of the mother more so than the father, so the thinking of society has been. And the mother has usually received custody of young children in divorce proceedings. If she has to provide housing, food, clothing, and other necessaries for herself while caring for the children, then alimony may be a must, if she's to get by at all with the care for herself and the children.

In some cases, such as when one of the children is physically or mentally handicapped, she may not be able to work outside the home in order to earn a living. In other cases she will not have been trained for a job that would provide income for secure living. In some cases the wife not only has no trade with which to make a living for herself but is reasonably too old to learn a trade in order to make a living. In other cases, the wife may be physically or mentally unable to work. In such cases it would be only fair and equitable that she receive alimony.

But, with the ERA, the chance of receiving alimony for the needy wife will become slim, and it likely will fade into nonexistence. The Movement is setting the tone, and the ERA will likely clinch it!

As the Movement demands more competition in man's world, the laws which will flow from the ERA will do away with the distinctions, social and economic and legal, between man and woman. The wife who was once given a special place in the "cold and cruel" world will no longer occupy this position.

She will be compelled to do the best which she can in making a living for herself and for her minor children. Although she may lack training and physical ability to do manual labor, she'll have to try it, if it's the only means of earning a living.

While the husband may be financially able to pay alimony, he may be one of those who won't, unless ordered by the court to do so.

As the law of the ERA results in a philosophy of doing away with femininity, the "ex" will not want any longer to recognize his "ex" as a person of femininity who needs special consideration in support of herself.

She'll be thought of as just another fellow in society, totally responsible for her own needs and survival.

Should the law of the ERA not immediately do away with alimony for a wife, the likelihood that it must eventually do so is sound, because, once the attitude of society is that woman now is treated as a man, the attitude will be to let her survive as a man. Her expectations will, to some extent, come to pass. Her expectation of being able to compete with man in a man's world may be fulfilled, in some respects, should the ERA become law. However, her expectations may not include having to be treated as a man and having to survive as a man, but such will be the case. For every right gained by the ERA, at least one or more duties will be gained, whether by choice or by law.

So, as such attitude spreads over society, so will the law. Law in our society which is not consistent with the will of the vast majority can little endure.

Law in our society is no better than the will of the people. While law which is inconsistent with the attitude or will of the people may momentarily restrain the people, it can't for long. Soon, such a law is either repealed or becomes unenforceable, worth only the physical space in which it's stored.

Also, like other legal issues, should the ERA become law, alimony will become subject to control by the federal courts which have neither the legal training nor knowledge of the local needs of the people in order to pass sound judgment in cases involving alimony.

However, as husbands and wives become unhappy by either receiving alimony, by receiving no alimony, or by receiving what will be thought to be not enough, they will yell, "discrimination based on sex!" Away to the federal courts they'll go, where not only alimony but all other legal issues of their cases will be subjected to control by these courts.

Who's to lose alimony if the ERA becomes law? The married woman will, of course! Since man has never had rights to alimony, until recently in some jurisdictions, he doesn't stand to lose. In fact, in many cases in which a husband would be required to pay alimony, he will no longer be required to do so, if the ERA becomes law, once the courts and legislatures start grinding away with laws which will have to be compatible with the ERA.

Nor does the single woman have anything to lose. Many women in this status are proponents of the ERA, who can't or don't expect to be married, happily married.

Proponents of the ERA have conceded that the ERA will undoubtedly do away with alimony for some wives who would receive it in cases involving legal separation or divorce. But the proponents reason that, women must give up something in exchange for passage of the ERA! So, alimony may as well be one of the things to give up.

How about the needy wife who legitimately needs alimony? Also, How about the husband and wife who might very well reconcile marital differences and live happily married, except that no legal obligation to pay alimony becomes an incentive for the husband to pursue a final divorce, letting emotions prevail over common sense because of hasty decisions triggered and placed into operation by inducement furnished under the laws of the ERA?

Too, How about the minor children who will be subjected to broken homes which could very well turn into happy homes for them, except that the incentive for divorce becomes too strong, arising from the hasty decisions triggered by the ERA?

These are questions which every proponent of the ERA should consider, long and hard!

We're not only talking about a needy wife losing support under the ERA, but also what the issue of alimony under the ERA will bring to bear upon the relations between husband and wife, upon the relations between parent and child, upon the relations among every member of a family, as well as future happiness for every member of a family.

Nor can we consider only that a few women may not be

affected by the issue of alimony under the ERA. More is at stake! We must consider the total effects of the issue of alimony to all members of our society.

To do otherwise would be to ignore the total structure of the family and how the family fits into the total structure of our society.

The issue of alimony will, if and when the ERA becomes law, be a contributory factor to disruption of relations between husband and wife, to disruption of relations between parent and child, as well as a contributory factor in an expected increase in the divorce rate, resulting in disintegration of the family as an institution in our society.

12

Child Support, Custody, and Visitation Rights

Not only can a wife expect to lose some legal rights to alimony in the event that the ERA becomes law but she can, if a mother, expect to lose some legal rights involving child support, custody of a minor child or children, and visitation rights, because ratification and adoption of the ERA as law will result in revolutionary changes in these areas, relationships between parents and a child or children.

Before discussing such changes, let's decide what these areas are, in a legal sense. Child support is the payment of money or other consideration or both by one party (usually the father) to another party (usually the mother) for the support and maintenance of the welfare of a child or children as required by a court of law in a case involving either a legal separation or divorce granted by the court.

The court can require that payments for child support be made weekly, monthly, or at any other intervals which the court feels are appropriate. Also, the court can, for good cause—such as changes in the financial conditions of the father or mother or changes in the needs of the child or children—change the sum of payments and the time for payments.

For example, as the child becomes older, needs may increase for clothing and for other matters; therefore, the court may require that the periodic sums of payments for support be increased. On the other hand, should the father who makes the payments lose his job, or take a mandatory cut in salary, or become sick and therefore unable to pay the required sum, the court can reduce the payments, as well as change the time when payments are to be made.

Keep in mind that the primary concern of the court is the welfare of the minor child or children and that the wishes, needs, rights, and duties of the father and mother are secondary to the welfare of the child or children in all matters which affect the child or children, such as support, custody, and visitation rights.

Once a court takes jurisdiction in matters which involve a minor child or children, the child or children become wards of the state, and, as such, the court is responsible for making sure that the child or children receive proper care and treatment at all times, to the exclusion of wishes and needs of the mother and father if necessary. This is the power which gives a court the right to take custody from both the mother and father if necessary and place the child or children in a foster home or with some other responsible party.

In considering the sum to be paid for child support, the court considers the financial ability of the party who is required to make payments, such as his income and owned assets, as well as the financial ability to contribute to the support of the child or children by the party who is to receive custody of them.

Also the customary living standards of the child or children are considered because a change in such standards, if drastic, may very well contribute to the emotional trauma of the child or children. For example, as a result of a legal separation or divorce between the parents, will the child be economically required to move from a middle-class home with the comforts of steak and milk and middle-class friends into a run-down shack with beans and water and lack of proper clothing and entertainment, away from old friends? Such a change in living standards for the child could very well be detrimental to the child's emotional stability, with which the court is highly concerned.

When there's either a legal separation or divorce granted by the court, the court must decide whether the mother or the father is to have possession of the minor child or children. The possession may be temporary or permanent, until further order of the court making any change in the possession. The party (usually the mother) who is awarded possession of the child or children is considered to have custody of the child or children, with authority to keep, maintain, and discipline them.

The other party (usually the father) is generally granted certain rights to visit with the minor child or children at certain times and on certain days or at times which are reasonable, depending on what the court decides will be appropriate for the particular case. The age of the child, the conveniences of the child, the conveniences for the father and the mother, and any other factor which the court deems proper may be considered when deciding what the times and dates for visitation shall be, keeping in mind that the welfare of the child or children is first and foremost.

While uncommon, a party may be denied any and all visitation rights if visitation with the child or children would be detrimental to their welfare. For example, a habitually alcoholic father or mother may be denied visitation rights by the court, if in the interest of the children.

As in the case of child support, for good cause, the court can change rights and duties in respect to both custody and visitation rights. For example, the court may take custody away from the mother and grant custody of the child or children to the father, in the event that the court decides that the mother has become unfit for custody.

Any party who violates the court's order in respect to these matters can be subjected to contempt of the court and, if found guilty of contempt, be fined or imprisoned or both. When the welfare of a minor child is at stake, a court is not reluctant to hold any or all parties in contempt when misconduct is proved to be in willful violation of the court's order.

Now, since we have some understanding of the legal meaning of child support, custody, and visitation rights, why will ratification and adoption of the ERA as law result in revolutionary changes in these areas?

Because, once the ERA becomes law, many mothers will lose rights to custody of minor children, and many fathers will gain rights to custody of minor children, and many mothers will become legally obligated to send child-support payments to fathers, discharging fathers from this traditional duty.

A fit mother has customarily and traditionally been granted permanent custody of the minor child or children, customarily and traditionally been awarded child support paid by the father, with the father customarily and traditionally receiving visitation rights to visit with the children. The mother has received custody of the child or children because she was a female. In other words, the mother's rights to both custody of minor children and child support payments from the father have been based on sex!

However, should the ERA become law, this preferential treatment based on sex will fly into the very teeth of the law which is supposedly a law to do away with discrimination based on sex.

Thus the rights which have been traditionally granted to a mother in cases of either legal separation or divorce in respect to custody and child support will cease to exist. Law is law, or it's not! The law can't be in favor of discrimination based on sex for the benefit of the mother or for the benefit of the children.

Will such a law as the ERA be fair and just and meet the needs of both minor children and parents in these cases?

Perhaps yes, in some cases, but perhaps no, in most cases. In light of the welfare of minor children as well as fairness for the mother and father such a cold-blooded law would not be appropriate for flexible needs of each and every peculiar case. Let's examine this proposition.

First, most experts in the field of child psychology as well as other persons experienced in areas of needs for minor children and parents in legal cases would likely agree that a child is in much greater emotional need of the mother than of the father, assuming that the mother is a fit mother, until the child is around twelve years of age.

The reasoning process is that, after birth, a child visually identifies with the mother, since she, not the father, is in constant contact with the child, and a child will experience anxiety when separated from the mother, with such separation causing emotional and social difficulties for the child later in life as well as during childhood.

Secondly, the mother is instinctively better equipped, that is, she has more natural and innate ability to deal with the child's emotional needs and growth than is true for the father.

Thirdly, the mother's occupation as a mother in the home

or even in her occupation outside the home usually has more regularity in respect to a time schedule than does a father's, and therefore she can provide more regularity to the needs of the child than can the father.

Fourthly, the father can fend for himself in the economic world better than can the mother; therefore, the father should earn money and send it to the mother for the child, which will allow the mother to care for the child.

These assumptions may not be sound in every respect and in every case when there's either a legal separation or a divorce. Yet, the courts have been rather consistent in a vast majority of cases in awarding custody of minor children to mothers and requiring fathers to pay child support.

It has been my experience as a lawyer that lawyers, judges, fathers, and mothers have seldom questioned a mother's right to custody of a rather young child or children in these cases.

All have always taken for granted that the mother would be entitled to custody, with no questions, unless she either expressed no desire for custody or the court found her to be unfit for custody, and, in order to be unfit for custody, the mother has had to be grossly neglectful of the child's or children's physical and mental welfare.

But, once the ERA becomes law, if it does, many fathers will challenge a mother's traditional rights to custody of minor children when there's either a legal separation or a divorce, as well as challenge a father's traditional duty to pay child support.

The courts can't let such challenges go unnoticed and unattended. Courts will be faced with this proposition: Either they will have to continue the tradition of granting custody of minor children to mothers and also requiring fathers to pay child support payments to mothers, or they will have to grant equal rights to fathers in cases involving custody and child support, as required by the ERA. In the latter situation, the courts will have to abandon the traditional rights for mothers in these cases. Thus, the revolutionary changes in these legal areas will confront the courts, should the ERA become law, and the courts must decide what to do.

Should courts ignore the ERA, if it becomes law, then respect for both the courts and law will be lost, and, in this event, the law will likely become unenforceable in due course of time, because when a majority of people in America have no respect for a law, the law is meaningless.

On the other hand, if courts ignore what has been traditionally thought to be in the best interests of both minor children and parents in cases involving a legal separation or a divorce, then, in this event, the needs of minor children as well as the proper needs of parents will suffer.

As the law now stands, without the ERA, in respect to powers of courts in cases involving either a legal separation or a divorce, the law is flexible enough to consider and meet the needs of all parties in a particular and peculiar case.

However, the proposed ERA will be a cold-blooded law if ratified and adopted because it will not allow for flexibility in considering and meeting the needs of minor children and parents in these cases. The ERA will not allow sex to be considered in meeting needs.

Yet, anyone who is experienced in these legal areas will readily admit that sex is a relevant factor when considering both the needs of children and parents. For example, a five-year-old daughter may need the attention and custody by the mother, while a fifteen-year-old son may need the attention and custody by the father.

Assuming that both the mother and father are equally fit for custody of these children, they would have equal rights to custody under the proposed ERA. Custody granted to the mother would result in an allegation of discrimination based on sex from the father, while custody granted to the father would result in the same allegation from the mother.

So, there you are! The ERA can't meet the peculiar needs of either minor children or parents. Its sole usefulness will be to allow the parents to use it as a legal tool for the purpose of harassing each other, resulting in mental turmoil to both the parents and minor children.

13

Emotional Growth and Stability for Children

So far, we've said little about the effects of the Movement and the proposed ERA on children. In any marriage and in any divorce, children are weighty and demanding factors for consideration. In any marriage and in any divorce, we can find the mold which shapes a young child's emotional security or insecurity, his or her happiness or unhappiness.

Like an adult, a child is a product of his or her environment.

While a happy relationship between a father and mother provides a healthy and happy environment which molds a child of the marriage to be mentally healthy, it's equally true that, on the other hand, an unhappy relationship between a father and mother molds the child to be insecure, afraid of life, frustrated, confused, and generally unhappy.

Such a relationship between the parents produces such a child, the happy or unhappy child, molded and carved by such an environment.

The mental state of a parent pretty well determines how the parent will care for and rear the child, and the kind of care given by the parent to the child will influence the nature of growth of the child. Thus, an emotionally stable parent will influence a child to become emotionally stable, while an emotionally unstable parent will influence a child to become emotionally unstable.

A child will, therefore, become, in growth, whatever he sees, feels, and learns from his or her parents, who direct and control the family life.

Especially in formative years of growth, the child knows and understands and accepts whatever is exposed to him or her

in the family environment. This is about the only environment
which the child knows and understands in formative years.
Hence, parents who display discord and conflict to the child will
educate the child accordingly. On the other hand, parents who
display peace and harmony to the child will educate the child accordingly. Whatever the child learns from the parents will shape
and mold the child's life, with lasting effects.

Therefore, the family is the most basic institution in our
society for developing the child's potential: emotional, moral,
intellectual, spiritual, as well as social and physical well-being.

It is within the family where the child accepts rules that
define the time, place, and circumstances under which personal
needs may be satisfied. It's the family which gives the child the
philosophy which will be used throughout life. Of course, the
father and mother are the family in the American way of life.
They determine just what the family, with its members, will or
will not be.

A parent is about the only guide in life during formative
years which a child has. And, whatever care the child receives
during these years will be his or her tools for working and getting along in life.

During these years, the stage is set in life for healthy, normal,
and interpersonal relations with others, or the stage is set
in life for conflict and discord in relations with others.

For example, during my years as a practicing attorney, I've
noticed that clients who have come to me for legal divorce were,
in many cases, products of an unhappy life while growing in the
home as a child. His or her parents didn't get along too well.
The emotional instability of the parents had become a permanent
part of the child's life, which was carried over into adult life,
then into the marriage. The person had become a duplicate of
his or her parents in respect to either emotional instability or
emotional stability.

The same process of reasoning can be applied to delinquent
or criminal behavior. Having been both criminal prosecutor and
defense attorney during my years of law practice, I've had the
opportunity to notice that unhappiness between parents increased

the likelihood that their children would commit delinquent or criminal behavior, more so than children from happy homes. The conclusion may be that marital discord exposed the child to delinquent or criminal influences, perhaps from a feeling of rejection, neglect, and lack of respect for parents, which feelings were transferred by the child to others in society, causing the child to run head-on into our criminal laws.

Failure of the unstable parent or parents to indoctrinate the child with normal, happy, and acceptable behavior had not prepared the child to cope with problems encountered in society.

Just as a painting becomes whatever an artist makes it, a child becomes whatever the parents make him or her. Just as a painting is no more or no less than the colors and methods and materials used by the artist, a child in formative years is no more or no less than the kind of care and understanding given by the parents to the child. A child is a product of formative years and will likely be pretty much the same product later in adult life.

So, a confusing and unhappy parent makes and molds a confusing and unhappy child who lives in unhappiness and passes it on to others, making the child somewhat of a misfit for adjustment to society.

This being the case, what do the philosophy and actions of the Movement, and the philosophy and actions to be reaped from the proposed ERA (if it becomes law) have to do with the emotional growth and stability of children?

First, we can assume that there will be discord and conflict between some fathers and mothers as a result of the philosophy and actions.

Second, we can assume that a child living with such a father and mother will be influenced by the discord and conflict between the parents, causing emotional disturbance for the child, thereby resulting in disturbed growth for normal and happy personality development for the child.

Let's look at some specific situations.

Let's take the physical and mental care of a young child, say from the time of birth until the child is about twelve years of age. Such care during this period has been the primary responsibility of the mother, where practical in the marriage. The Movement wishes, however, to relieve a mother of this responsibility, as pointed out in chapter 2 by Gloria Steinem who thinks that a mother should not be required to stay home and care for a child, but if so, no more so than should the father.

First, the popular and accepted view is that a rather young child needs the care of the mother more so than the father's care, and there seems to be much truth in this as we pointed out in the preceding chapter.

Of course, for many families, either the father or mother or both must earn an economic living for the family, and since a father usually has a greater earning capacity than does a mother and since a child needs the mother's care more than that of the father, then the father is the one who should get out and earn a living for the family.

Second, a mother who objects to staying home and caring for the child or children may likely have a poor attitude toward such care while caring for them.

And the worst thing is, that the child can sense a feeling of rejection in this situation, causing the child to feel unwanted and therefore insecure. Such feeling may very well go with the child throughout life, causing the child to live in a state of conflict and discord which was learned from the parents as a result of poor attitude and improper care for the child. The child's insecure feeling could very well result in disruption and retardation of normal emotional growth and stability for the child because a sense of security is generally necessary to normal growth and stability.

Also the mother who seeks to compete in ways and occupations which have been pretty much in a man's world will, first, be unable to devote proper time and attention to the care for a minor child or children at home and, second, will likely evoke her husband's counterattacks to her refusal or failure to care for the child or children, unless justified by economic necessity.

In either case, there's likely to be conflict and discord between the mother and father, causing frustrated and insecure relations between them, which in turn will be observed and felt by their minor child or children.

In this situation the child or children will learn and adopt the frustration and insecurity which exist between the parents, and a child can't achieve normal growth and happiness and therefore a well-adjusted personality, when living in frustration and insecurity. Such an environment is likely to ingrain a deep sense of fear in the child, which will likely become a permanent part of the child's personality as a result of the learning process provided for the child by the parents.

Keep in mind that a child, like an adult, will register impressions of whatever is seen, felt, and communicated to the child in any manner. This is especially true for a child in formative years, because during this period a child is very receptive to his or her surroundings.

What happens to a child when the father loses interest in the wife and mother? In such a case the effects for the child are not likely to be good. The wife and mother who adopts and practices the philosophy and actions of the Movement will likely lose her husband's interest in love for her, affection for her, respect for her, and mutual help and understanding for her. Such lack of interest will likely result in a breakdown of the marriage.

As the relations between them deteriorate for lack of these things which are so necessary to a healthy and harmonious marriage, their child or children will also observe and feel the need for these things, because, as we've said, the care and attitude between the parents will be the care and attitude which the child or children will learn and adopt, causing a void feeling for love and security for the child or children.

Without proper love, proper understanding, and proper care and attention between the parents, the parents can't live in peace and harmony in the home, and if these things don't exist in the home the child or children who live in the home are also without these things which are essential to normal development and growth for them.

Remember, a child's primary learning environment in formative years for the child is in the home which is directed and controlled by the parents. Whatever the child sees, hears, feels, and the way in which he or she is treated by the parents will determine what kind of person the child will become, a person who is emotionally stable and happy or a person who is emotionally frustrated, living in fear and unhappiness.

Then there's the issue of femininity. A daughter who is socialized and internalized by her mother's lack of femininity in the home will grow into adulthood without much knowledge and understanding of femininity. The impressions which the daughter receives about her mother will likely become the mold which carves and determines the daughter's attitude of her own self-image of femininity.

Without a good self-image of her capability in femininity, the daughter may very well encounter some rather difficult times as a wife and mother because, as our society now stands, femininity for a woman is a highly desired quality for becoming a desirable wife and mother. All you have to do as a woman to understand this is to begin a search for a prospective husband! Also you may as a woman want to observe a wife who is happily married.

Too, a son who has grown into manhood without knowledge and respect for femininity in a woman's world can't have respect for femininity, once married, although such respect is vital to the needs and desires of any well-adjusted wife. To be respected and treated as a woman of femininity is the dream of every well-adjusted woman.

Like the daughter, the son knows and gives to others what he has primarily learned from the parents in the home, whether it be love and respect and understanding of femininity or resentment and rejection and ignorance of the importance of femininity to a wife.

A daughter and son will usually give to their marriages, when reaching this stage, a good bit of what they primarily learned about the marriage of their parents.

For example, a son or daughter who grows up in a home where a happy and successful marriage prevails is more likely to give the care and understanding necessary for his or her happy and successful marriage than would be true, had he or she lived in a childhood home where the marriage of the parents was a failure or near failure because of conflict and discord between the parents.

This is true because the daughter's or son's attitude about marriage is, to a large extent, shaped and determined by the conditions experienced in his or her parents' marriage. Thus, in many cases, the daughter's or son's marriage will become a duplicate of her or his parents' marriage.

Negative and doubtful behavior of the parents' marriage on the one hand, or positive and creative behavior on the other hand, is the behavior socialized and internalized by the son or daughter, and such behavior will be a very influential factor in shaping and determining the daughter's or son's marriage.

The same is true for sexual relations learned by the daughter or son in the parents' home. An attitude about sexual relations will be learned by a son or daughter, based on what is observed about the parents' actions toward each other, what they did or did not do in respect to their affections or lack of affections. An attitude will be formed even though the children have had no education about sex presented by the parents. Love, patience, and affectionate understanding give a child some understanding of an impression about sexual relations between the parents, as does resentment, bickering, and jealous competition.

The Movement seems to preach that woman has too long been used by man for sexual purposes and for the purpose of bearing a child for man, making a woman a slave to the selfish wishes and needs of man, to the exclusion of the needs of a woman to be more than a servant to man. Such an attitude is not consistent with pleasant and compatible sexual relations between parents where the wife chooses to adopt and practice such an attitude.

Sexual relations are, if successful, like any other relations between parents, strictly voluntary, from mutual desire, willingly total submission to each other without conditions!

Therefore, to create rejection or resentment toward sexual relations between parents as a tool to be used by the philosophy and actions of the Movement for the purpose of doing away with femininity in order to destroy distinctions between a man and woman is negative and dangerous philosophy for a daughter or son to learn and adopt.

This is true because a marriage is not likely to be successful unless a wife and husband can openly, joyfully, and with total and unconditional submission search and learn and enjoy compatible sexual relations.

And this is not possible if the wife is going to use sex as a weapon to whip her husband into her way of supposedly being equal to him, an objective of the Movement. Such use of sex will only make life miserable for a marriage, likely leading to a separation or divorce.

For sons or daughters to be exposed to conflict and discord in respect to sexual relations as well as to all other relations between parents will not prepare them for a sense of peace, a sense of tolerance, a philosophy of calmness, and a sense of mutual understanding, which things will be necessary for their own marriage if they are to be successful.

Having been subjected to conflict and discord between the parents, a son or daughter may very well use and apply these negative conditions to his or her own marriage, either consciously or unconsciously, leading the marriage to problems involving divorce, alimony, child support, and custody of his or her minor child or children.

Such problems will in many cases cause the son or daughter to experience disintegration of his or her own marriage and family, as we shall further see in chapter 15.

Another area which will cause tension, conflict, discord, and fear for children is the experience of legal battles between the parents as a result of conditions brought about by the philosophy and actions of the Movement, as we discussed in chapter 3, if the ERA becomes law.

Such tension, conflict, discord, and fear can and will not only become a part of a daughter's or son's personality but will be passed on to his or her child or children.

Should it become law, the ERA can and will be used as a

tool by many parents in any disagreement which may arise in the marriage, all in the name of equality of rights, whether such use of the law is founded on solid ground or founded on whim and caprice for the purpose of venting frustration arising from the philosophy and actions of the Movement.

Such troubles will shape and mold the lives of children for both the present and for the future, once the full effects of the Movement are felt.

The experience of mental disorder of parents, harassment between them, and the division between them brought about by the Movement will build a foundation of mental disorder and discontentment for the children who see, feel, and live in these conditions which exist between parents.

Children living in these conditions will experience maladjustment in emotional growth and stability because the personality development of a child, shaped in formative years, is a reflection of attitudes and practices learned from the parents.

The attitudes and practices of the parents will, to a large extent in many cases, be adopted by the child or children because whatever the child or children are exposed to by the parents is about the only learning environment for them during their formative years.

Thus the attitudes and practices of conflict and discord between the parents will lend a learning experience of insecurity, fear, and frustration to the child. With such feelings, a child can't expect to attain the emotional growth and stability necessary to a normal and happy life, because the child can't expect to be much more than a product of his or her environment provided by the parents.

14

Increase in the Divorce Rate

The philosophy and actions of the Movement will quickly increase the already increasingly large divorce rate in the American society, and the divorce rate will be further accelerated by the ERA, if it becomes law.

This is so because, through its philosophy and actions, the Movement will change the life-style in marriage, or attempt to do so, which will cause conditions and grounds, coupled to desire, for divorce.

More than any other single factor, the philosophy and actions of the Movement will lead man and woman to enter into marriage with a skeptical and cynical attitude about each other and about their marriage.

The woman who enters into marriage with the internalization of the philosophy and actions of the Movement and who attempts to institutionalize the marriage with such philosophy and actions is preoccupied with "self-fulfillment" for women, the argument advanced by the Movement.

She sees and feels that "self-fulfillment" is inconsistent with the normal role of wife, inconsistent with the normal role performed by a husband, inconsistent with giving birth to children and caring for them, inconsistent with maintaining a home and family, if such should in any way lead to performance of the traditional role as wife, and she is dead set with the idea of making sure that she is equal to her husband, and that she is afforded the same and equal opportunity which he has in all social and economic aspects of life!

Knowing and sensing the attitude of his bride, the groom enters into the marriage with about the same skeptical and cynical attitude held by his wife, to be applied to his wife, to himself, and to the marriage.

So both enter and begin to live the marriage with the secret feeling and aims that, "If it doesn't work out, I'll get a divorce!" Such attitude in marriage can little endure in a successful and happy marriage.

At this point the stage for marriage is set, the mind has been programmed, the actions will come! The divorce court is just around the corner.

And the divorce court will likely be sought and used, not only by the couple who enters the marriage with such skeptical and cynical attitude derived from the philosophy and actions of the Movement but by the couple who acquires and practices the philosophy and actions of the Movement after becoming married.

A woman's adoption and practice of the philosophy and actions of the Movement in marriage will lead to venting frustration and resentment toward her husband who will, in turn, respond to her with more frustration and more resentment. Such attitude and conduct between them will build and lead to mountains of hostile and unfriendly competition in the marriage, one trying to win over the other in destructive criticism and degradation.

Each will pounce on the other with both words and actions of belittlement, words and actions of ugly disparagement, words and actions which will test the very ability to remain sane!

The time will come when the wife is always ready to wage war against the husband and when the husband is always ready to wage war against the wife. One will mentally tug and mentally tear at the other!

The pain of living in the marriage will become unbearable, and so the statistics in the divorce rate will rise.

Yes, such will be the case for those in marriage who practice the philosophy and actions of the Movement, because the philosophy and actions don't tolerate freedom for mutual help in marriage, mutual love in marriage, mutual and yet independent growth in individualities of husband and wife, for the philosophy and actions of the Movement are solely concerned with the development of a life-style in marriage which will allow a woman to decide when, where, and how she should build and maintain a structure in marriage for the sole purpose of being conducive to "equality for women."

And the sad and unfortunate part of the philosophy and actions is that the structure is to be erected and maintained by arrogant independence and anti-male beliefs, at least and until the structure has met the specifications advocated by the Movement!

Thus, the life-style in marriage advocated by the Movement is neither desirable nor workable for a happy and successful marriage.

Being derived from the philosophy and actions of the Movement, the life-style in marriage will breed contempt and distrust in the marriage, because such philosophy and actions hold that man has oppressed woman, suppressed woman, and made woman subservient to man, and that he is likely to continue to do so unless compelled by law to do otherwise, one of the Movement's objectives in the proposed passage of the ERA.

Hence the wife who believes in the philosophy and actions of the Movement is likely to transfer her negative feelings about men to her husband, a feeling of contempt and distrust, not in every case but in many.

So contempt and distrust will breed more contempt and distrust in the marriage, and the end products of contempt and distrust are fear, restraint, uneasiness, resentment and despair.

The husband and wife will, being under pressure of such conditions, be afraid to repose faith, confidence, and freedom of actions and words in each other, with contempt and distrust permeating the very fiber and environment of the marriage. For most marriages which exist with such conditions, divorce is the end product.

One must conclude that the Movement is driven by leadership which is lacking knowledge and understanding of how to influence and win men! Further, one must conclude that the leadership of the Movement is either unaware of or in some way fails to realize that the goal of nearly every well-adjusted woman, if not everyone, is to live in a happy marriage, and also that the leadership doesn't understand or refuses to recognize that neither a husband nor a wife can force each other by law to love, respect, and care for the marriage or care for each other.

Whatever good that exists in a marriage is a result of mutual respect, mutual care, mutual love, mutual tolerance, and mutual understanding.

Such accomplishments in marriage can never be realized when a wife or a husband or both are under a constant, unfriendly and competitive spirit, with distrust always lurking and prowling in the mind.

No! No happy and livable life-style in marriage can ever be accomplished by the present philosophy and actions of the Movement. The belligerancy and rebellion offered by the Movement to a wife for use in her marriage are the very last things which could possibly and favorably influence her husband!

The Movement tells her to belligerantly rebel against bearing children, if to do so would hurt the image of the Movement's cause; to belligerantly rebel against staying home and looking after the children while her husband pursues his occupation outside the home; to insist that the wife do no more than one-half of cleaning the house, washing dishes, cooking, and staying home and looking after the children because to do otherwise would make her less than equal to her husband; and, above all, to never forget that her husband is a man and that, as such, belongs to the group which has deceptively and connivingly shared in making woman subservient to and unequal to man!

The Movement says that all social, economic, and political recognition is not to be shared by less than fifty percent for the wife, because any figure less than fifty percent would upset the balance of equality between her and her husband!

In addition, by all means, she should never be feminine because femininity has resulted in one of man's ways in paying special recognition and special protection to a woman's world, and it's this very recognition and protection which help to greatly make a distinction between man and woman!

Man should never be attracted to woman because she is feminine since, to do so, would be to use sex as a means of discriminating against women!

The Movement says to do away with identity as wife, identity as a person of femininity, and place the Great Cause of the Movement above husband, above child, and above marriage, and to always remember that the one great and uncompromising loyalty of women is first to the Movement's cause, and that anything left over may be advanced to the use of finding happiness in marriage, in happily rearing children, and in happily existing as husband and wife.

So goes the life-style for marriage and family, as presented by the Movement, which can only result in an increase in the divorce rate in the American society.

True, each man and woman should have the free choice in choosing how he or she will live the marriage, including this choice for the leaders of the Movement.

But with the Movement, the matter of free choice is not to be considered, because the Movement seeks to force its beliefs on others, to be practiced by others, and to be hopefully enforced against others by the ERA if it happens to become law.

Free choice in style of marriage is not, if in conflict with the philosophy and actions of the Movement, to be tolerated, since freedom and tolerance which are inconsistent with the philosophy and actions of the Movement are abhorrent to the Movement's Great Cause!

While in some marriages divorce may be the only reasonable alternative to the solution for problems of the marriages, yet many marriages will, however, result in divorce caused by the philosophy and actions of the Movement, which marriages could otherwise be turned into lasting and happy ones.

Many women will, either intentionally or unintentionally, be adversely influenced by the teachings of the Movement. And if the ERA becomes law, many women will use it as a tool to vent personal frustration at their husbands, thereby adding to the increase in the divorce rate. While there are a few exceptions, most husbands and wives will rush for a divorce when they start suing each other under the ERA.

Remember, a person can file a lawsuit against another, although there may be no proper or reasonable ground for filing the lawsuit, and there may be no grounds whatsoever. However, once the lawsuit is filed, the damage is done! While the lawsuit may never be pursued to a final conclusion of the possible legal merits, once an unfriendly lawsuit is filed by a husband against a wife, or by a wife against her husband, the chance of ever reconciling differences for a possibly happy marriage is nearly, if not totally, nonexistent.

You may say, "So what! The divorce rate is increased by the Movement?"

For those who have worked in domestic relations involving divorce, the answer is obvious, but less obvious for those who lack this experience.

A divorce does, in reality, dissolve the family group, usually adversely affecting the lives of the children and the wife and the husband, as well as adversely affecting the social and economic stability of all members of the family. Usually a divorce has by-products of deep and lasting traumatic experiences for all concerned, such as emotional shock, economic problems, and social stigma.

So, for the Movement to advocate philosophy and actions which will abolish the American family as an institution by an increase in the divorce rate, such result to be codified and enforced by the ERA if it becomes law, should be a serious matter for all of us. More will be said about this in the next chapter.

15

Abolishment of Family

What would you say if I told you that the present philosophy and actions of the Women's Liberation Movement will contribute to the abolishment of the family as an institution in our American society, and that such abolishment of the family will in effect be legalized and enforced by the ERA if it becomes law?

What would your daughter or your son be without a family—without a mother, without a father, and without a home, which is part of the family? What would you be, today, had you not had a family and if you didn't have a family at the present time to enjoy? What would society be without the family as an institution?

Can you think of any phase of American life—love, professions, businesses, marriage, religion, sex, or any other part of American life, that is not more influenced by the family as an institution than by anything else?

Everything in our society revolves around the family. The family is the nucleus of all activity in our society, whether social, economic, or political. All activities are made and geared for serving the needs of the family. The goals and purposes of the family take priority over all else in our form of society. Ask any man or woman, "Does your family come first?"

The answer is likely to be yes in every situation. The family is placed above country, above profession, above business, above friends, and above all other stations or things in our society, as a general rule.

This is the thinking and actions of the culture in our society. It's the strong feeling with which we're socialized from the time of birth—the way we're taught, the way we think, and the way we act.

One's first process of learning takes place in the family which makes up the family home. It's here where a child first learns to think, to talk, to listen, and to look. It's the family which teaches the child to first learn to develop the intellect, to develop in social and in all other areas of life. It's here where the child first learns to act and to react to persons and to situations.

It's the family in which a child learns to love, learns to be loved, and learns to mature to a point at which the child can grow and fend for himself or herself.

Take away the family, and what does a child have? Without the family, the child cannot survive, either physically or mentally.

For that matter, what would a man have without a wife, without a home, and without children? Or, what would a woman have without a home, without a husband, and without children? We're talking about the vast majority of both men and women.

The family protects and cares for its members. It provides a setting in which not only can its members be protected but which provides approval of ways for the satisfaction of sexual drives, for reproduction of human life, and therefore for the approved surety of the perpetuation of society.

It's the family which provides stability for society—socially, economically, and politically. The very thread which holds society together is the family institution.

Without the family as an institution, society would have no order and no organization and no purpose, and, without such, people would run wild, without reason or purpose in and for life. Rights and duties would be replaced by chaos in society without the family as an institution. Some members of our society don't have families, but even these members look to and use the principles of the family as a barometer for proper living.

And yet, even in light of the unparalleled and paramount function of the family, the Movement's philosophy and actions will destroy or abolish the family as an institution, to a great extent, if the Movement is allowed to go unchecked and unrestrained.

What are the philosophy and actions of the Movement which would abolish the family? Let's discuss some of them.

Many of the Movement's supporters, the staunch ones, advocate doing away with legalized marriage. They say that man and woman should have society's approval, unblemished, to live together and give birth to children without being legally married, if they so desire. While such arrangement might be workable in some cases, it would not in a vast majority of cases. Why is this so?

Without being legally married, where is the status which would give the man and the woman a sense of responsibility—sexually, socially, and economically, to each other? Without legalized marriage, such man and woman are likely to abandon any sense of responsibility when winds of troubles between them start blowing. On the other hand, a legalized marriage will cause them to have a mutual feeling of social and legal responsibility.

In a legal marriage, they are apt to think, act, and take on responsibilities of a family. It's the family image which gives to them a feeling and need for survival, survival together.

It's also the family image, when sanctioned by a lawful marriage, which gives to them a sense of being responsible to their offspring, their child or children. It's the legalized marriage which causes the father and mother to willingly, or unwillingly required by law, provide for the needs of their children.

Without a legalized marriage, responsibility to offspring is hard to pin down by law, and it's impossible in some cases when there's denial of paternity.

So it's in the legalized family where the mother and father and child find security and stability and purpose in life.

Nor will communal living, which is advocated by many in the Movement, provide for a family setting which affords love, affection, protection, and responsibility of man to woman and woman to man and parent to child.

Such living does not provide closeness in love, affection, and purpose which are necessary in order to give desire and action to relations among mother, father and child. Communal living is too impersonal for unity and purpose found only in a family setting which consist of father, mother, and child. Freedom and responsibility in a family setting will not survive when daily shared and dictated by others outside the family, which would be the case, to some extent, in communal living.

Perhaps the most damaging to the survival of the family as an institution is the philosophy and actions, widespread in the Movement, which advocate that the wife and mother should no longer feel the desire and need to be identified as wife and mother and perform the roles of such personality. In fact, the Movement suggests that woman should rebel against the roles and image of wife and mother, because it's this image and these roles which the Movement says make the big distinction between man and woman and which force a woman to a subservient role, denying all rights and needs and equality to her, which in turn deny to her the need and right to "self-fulfillment."

Yet, I ask, What husband and what child really believe the Movement's proposition to be true? Further, What well-adjusted and happy wife and mother really believes the proposition to be true?

Very few, if any people (and I feel that no mature and happy person who believes and supports the family as an institution) can believe and support the Movement's proposition. Very few, if any, husbands and children who are also happy and well-adjusted would have any feeling but love and respect for the wife and mother who performs well and is happy in such roles.

A good image as wife and mother is perhaps the strongest link which holds a family together. The wife and mother is the very person who is idolized in the family, more so than any other member of the family.

To destroy such an image will destroy the family. Without this good image, the mother and wife will receive little respect from either the husband or child, unless she is forced to abandon the image by circumstances beyond her control. When respect for her goes, so will some love, some affection, and some voluntary responsibility to her.

It's the image of wife and mother which implants a sense of womanhood in a woman, from the time when she is a little girl old enough to sense and see and feel femininity; it's this sense and feeling of womanhood to which she takes pride in attaching her star in life. It's womanhood which gives to her a goal and purpose in life.

When the image of womanhood is taken from a woman, she will then consider herself a failure. And this is exactly what the philosophy and actions of the Movement will do, with the anti-male philosophy and resentment toward man.

Such actions and philosophy will cause a girl to grow up resenting man, resenting marriage, resenting children, resenting the role of wife and mother, resenting the role of husband and father, and eventually to resent herself, with nothing left for her but wonder and bewilderment in life.

This reasoning is equally true for man in respect to manhood. Every boy looks to and cherishes the day when he can fulfill manhood, which is primarily being a fine father and a fine husband and having a fine wife and fine children.

But his goals in manhood cannot be realized without womanhood, because one can't exist without the other, just as offspring can't come into being without both man and woman.

So, take away womanhood, and then manhood will be taken away; take both away, and the family will be taken away.

Without strong and permanent institutionalization of need and desire for womanhood and for manhood, why or how would a woman or a man feel the need and desire to enjoy and take on the responsibilities of a family? They wouldn't, because in our society one doesn't do very well or last very long in a situation in which he or she neither knows nor respects. Such situation, including a family, he or she will not tolerate for long.

Also there's the role of sexual satisfaction which will be adversely affected by the philosophy and actions of the Movement. It's quite true that a husband and wife are happiest in marriage when there's compatibility in sexual activity, but, How can there be compatibility in such activity between a man and woman when one or both are bickering, nagging, and constantly engaging in unfriendly and frustrated resentment toward each other, one fussing and fuming because she or he allegedly has an unfair and unequal role in the marriage?

Win or Lose?

When such an attitude exists in a marriage, there's likely to be little compatibility in sexual roles, and, if the attitude continues to exist, there's likely to be no sexual activity at all between them, then no marriage, then no family!

When on bad terms and therefore unhappy with each other for long, a husband and wife will grow not only to despise sexual relations between them, but to despise the marriage and to despise home life together, and they will not remain for long as a family.

In connection with sex, the Movement says that neither a husband nor the law should have any say as to whether or not a wife should seek an abortion, that the decision to have, or not to have, an abortion should be left to the sole judgment of the woman. However, it is submitted that a pregnant wife is carrying the makings of a human being which belong not only to her but also to her husband, assuming that he is responsible for the pregnancy. If you please, it's a situation of jointly owned property between husband and wife, which can't be destroyed without the consent of both!

To have an abortion without the husband's consent will lead to marital problems in the family in many cases, which could result in divorce and thus dissolution of the family.

Sole judgment for a wife in deciding as to whether or not she will have an abortion is part of the overall philosophy of the Movement, which advocates that a wife (as well as the divorced or single woman) should have sole discretion in all matters which affect her mind and body, independent of any consideration for the husband and children of the marriage, and that such is required if she is to seek and have "self-fulfillment."

How can there be "self-fulfillment" for a wife who fails to have a happy family, a happy husband, and happy children?

Reasonable independence and growth of individuality are necessary for a wife as well as for a husband and child, but certain rights and certain duties in a family must be considered and shared by all members of a family when the rights and duties affect all members of a family. Without such consideration, problems and unhappiness will arise which may make life miserable for the wife as well as for other members of the family.

A family as well as any other group must have mutuality in consideration of matters when they affect the individuals of the family or the individuals of the group. Otherwise, the family or group will fall apart for lack of both interest and participation by all individuals in common causes which affect them.

The economics, the social well-being, the education, the religion, the morality, and other matters concerning all members of the family must be considered and pursued as common goals for the benefit of the family as a successful unit. All things can't be considered for the sole benefit of the wife or for the sole benefit of the husband or for the sole benefit of the children. The welfare of one affects the welfare of all. Any other approach will likely dissolve the family in many cases.

To make matters worse for the stability and survival of the family, the ERA will, if made law, be used to assert alleged rights, to assert legal threats, and to file lawsuits by wives against husbands and by husbands against wives, using children as tools in the legal processes, for the purpose of venting frustration caused by the philosophy and actions of the Movement.

Thus, under such conditions, the Movement will be responsible for loss of freedom to maintain and enjoy life in a happy family—a loss for wives, a loss for husbands, and a loss for children.

16

Loss of Freedom

Freedom is the most precious of all human rights. It's more valuable and precious than all the gold and all the silver and all other material things, because these things are worthless without the freedom of personal choice to use them.

And far more precious than freedom to have and to control material things is one's freedom in his family affairs, in his marriage, in relations with his children, in other personal associations, and in his beliefs. Life in every respect is meaningless without freedom.

Law can be the guarantor and protector of freedom. On the other hand, law can and sometimes does take away the very freedom which it is supposed to give and protect. This will be the case with the ERA if it becomes law, because it will not allow for freedom in many areas of one's life.

How would you like for a stranger to meddle and interfere in and control your personal life, your life with your wife or husband, your life with your children, your personal life in your home, your life in your religion, and your life in your profession or business?

These are areas in which you generally expect absolute freedom, areas in which neither persons nor government should touch or meddle or control in any respect. And yet, these are areas in which the ERA will interfere and control to a great extent, should it become law.

While we've briefly discussed some of the expected loss of freedom as a result of the ERA, should it become law, in previous chapters, in this chapter we will further discuss areas in an attempt to tie up loose ends and summarize.

Your personal freedom in private life as well as in public life will be greatly diminished should the ERA become law. In many ways, all will become servants and slaves as the Movement's tools, if the ERA is ratified by a sufficient number (thirty-eight) of the state legislatures.

Remember, every law places some restraint on and takes away some personal freedom. No one will question our need for laws in certain areas of our lives, those areas in which laws are genuinely needed. On the other hand, it's hard for anyone to agree, after reasonable reflection, that the ERA could become a law which is or could be needed for any legitimate purpose.

The ERA will, if it becomes law, destroy the very things which the Movement says it is intended to provide and secure and protect: freedom to have equality. In fact, there will be neither equality nor freedom provided by the ERA.

This is true, because the ERA will not allow for personal choice in personal affairs, as well as in public affairs, nor will the ERA provide for solutions to problems based on equality, impartiality, fairness, needs, and qualifications.

To the contrary, the ERA will be interpreted and enforced with disregard for equality, since its very aim is to take away the rights of some and give them to others. In the end, the rights of all persons will be taken away. Just as surgery used to save life will end life, so will the ERA, used to provide equality, be the very law which will destroy equality.

Just like the Civil Rights laws, which have been interpreted and enforced without regard for equality and needs of the people in many respects, but concerned themselves solely with and enforced on the theory of "racially balanced integration," so will the ERA have no regard for freedom and needs of the people but will be solely concerned with "sexually balanced integration," thereby taking away personal choice and personal freedom of the people in their personal lives as well as freedom in public life.

You'll remember that in chapter 4 we discussed the Movement's main purpose in having the ERA as law, which is to treat sex by the courts as a "suspect classification." This means that once a woman has been denied or refused a demand, the courts are supposed to presume that such demand was denied or refused because she was a woman, based on sex discrimination, in other words.

Also, another primary purpose in having the ERA as law is to require that all activities, economically, socially, and otherwise, fill a certain quota of all positions with women, and this will be done without regard to needs and qualifications, just as has been the case in race-discrimination laws.

So where is the freedom? The equality? There can't be either with the ERA being interpreted and enforced in order to meet such aims.

For example, with the ERA as law, employers in private business as well as those in public business will be expected to fill quotas with a certain number of women in employment. The private employer who has to obtain a city license or a county license or a state license or a federal license will have sufficient government sanction of the business in order to come within the jurisdiction and enforcement of the ERA.

Too, if his services or goods are directly or indirectly subject to interstate commerce, which includes about all goods and services nowadays, this also will give sufficient government authority to interfere with classes of persons employed by him, including classes based on sex.

He will not have personal freedom to decide his needs, to decide what persons are qualified to fulfill those needs, because he will be required to hire a certain number of women, regardless of whether or not they are qualified and can fulfill his needs in employment, just as he has been required to hire a certain quota of persons of minority races without regard to needs and qualifications.

Once the ERA becomes law, he may be subjected to a lawsuit based on sex discrimination when he fails to hire or promote a woman.

Not only will he likely face a lawsuit in such cases, but he may very well be examined and inspected and harassed and threatened by government bureaucrats who will be armed with volumes of regulations and powers for the purpose of overseeing

and enforcing the ERA, just as has been the case in laws based
on race-discrimination situations.

If the ERA becomes law, both the business and professional
man will be faced with problems which will run something like
this: When he refuses to hire a woman or to promote a female
employee, he'll answer the door and find standing before him
members of—shall we say the Commission on Equality for Rights
Based on Sex, who will show their credentials and demand to
examine and inspect his books on hiring and firing practices for
the last ten years. In addition, the members will talk to his
employees, talk to his neighbors, talk to his business and professional associates about him, and talk to others, which may
result only in unjustified and unfair defamation of his character
and business or profession.

Members of the commission may find that he has five hundred positions for employees, filled with four hundred men and
only one hundred women.

The wrong quota! The court decisions and implementing
federal statutes, as well as the regulations of the commission, in
keeping with the intent of the ERA, now require that he fill the
five hundred positions with three hundred fifty men and one
hundred fifty women.

Never mind the lack of availability of qualified women for
employment and the men who are presently working for him,
just fill the positions with the proper ratio of men to women!
The business must be sexually balanced!

The employer and his attorney reject, in part, the demanded
recommendations of the Commission on Equality for Rights Based
on Sex. The commission files a lawsuit seeking damages, plus
attorney's fees and costs, and a restraining order from the court
closing the business by a certain day, unless the employer fully
complies with the commission's recommendations, of course, done
pursuant to the ERA!

Bad! Of course, but the employer's problems with the commission and with the court are not all. By now, the Movement
has hustled up several hundred women to protest, demonstrate,
and lead a boycott against the business.

At this point, the employer is on the brink of bankruptcy! But the bureaucrats of the commission, the Attorney General of the United States who is prosecutor of the employer, the Movement, and the court won't give up! Justice in the name of the ERA must be had against the employer!

So, the employer finds his business ruined, which sorry condition have spilled over into his marriage, into his family, and to the personal life of every member of his family, and he has now a bad reputation in his community for supposedly being a violator of law and an enemy of equality.

If only he had freedom! But his freedom was jerked away and destroyed by the laws of the ERA, all in the name of Equality of Rights!

Like the private and personal businesses, all personal and private as well as public clubs and associations will have to be sexually balanced pursuant to the ERA if it becomes law. They can't have all men or all women or all boys or all girls.

Nor can they have a ratio of males to females, if the ratio does not meet the requirements established by government bureaucrats, who will be armed with the power and authority for being sole judge as to what is to be a legal and proper ratio of men to women or boys to girls.

Remember, Big Brother—the government—knows best! And your personal freedom and your knowledge and your rights and your needs are not to interfere with Big Brother.

Under the ERA, it will be solely up to Big Brother to decide how many males and how many females will be in the Girl Scout clubs, in the Boy Scout clubs, in the Jaycees, in the Shriners, and in every other private and public association.

The sole aim under the ERA will be to have every association or group or organization composed of a legally required sexually balance of males to females.

Needs, desires, and rights of the members will not be considered if such will be inconsistent with the notions of the enforcer of the ERA.

Never mind freedom! It must fall. Everyone and everything must be computerized in accordance with sexually balanced integration pursuant to the ERA. Regardless of all needs and desires and rights, the fight for sexually balanced integration must go on!

The reasoning for sexually balanced integration in businesses, in professions, and in private and public clubs and associations will apply to all schools and all colleges and universities. Along with a present troublesome racial balance for schools, colleges, and universities will be a troublesome and accelerated spread of sexually balanced integration if the ERA becomes law.

School boards, school and college administrators, state legislatures, parents, students, and faculty members presently have little freedom in operating schools and colleges and universities. But, if the ERA becomes law, the little remaining freedom will vanish.

The institutions of learning have already been pretty much federalized. While present laws governing sexually balanced integration of schools and colleges and universities are sweeping in effects, since the institutions are subject to federal control primarily because they receive federal funds, the ERA will open the door to unlimited federalized control of the institutions. This will be the case, because the ERA will become a basic law for mandatory and computerized sexually balanced integration in respect to all areas in all schools and colleges and universities, notwithstanding federal funds. The pressure of federal authorities on schools and colleges and universities by use of federal funds as a tool will no longer be needed if and when the ERA becomes law. The ERA will be a sufficient tool to put any kind and degree of pressures on the institutions by federal authorities.

The ERA will, if it becomes law, strip the little remaining freedom of parents, state legislatures, students, administrators, and school boards in the operations of schools and colleges and universities. All operations and control of these institutions will quickly come under the sole determination of government bureaucrats and federal courts, more so than we presently have.

While we have sexually balanced integration in schools and colleges and universities as well as in other areas of life, present laws are, however, somewhat specific in application in most areas. This will not be the case if the ERA becomes law, because it will be broad enough and far-reaching enough to cover any and all areas of life in respect to sexually balanced integration.

This is why the Movement is anxious to have the ERA passed, so that the theory of "suspect classification" based on sex will apply to every situation. Put another way, any demand of a woman which is denied or refused in any area of life will give rise to alleged sex discrimination under the ERA. On the other hand, with the present laws, she must prove that she is entitled to relief under a specific law.

Private and public businesses, professions, associations, clubs, schools, colleges, and universities are not the only areas of American life which will be computerized by government standards for sexually balanced integration if the ERA becomes law. There's the area of religion and personal beliefs.

Under the ERA, churches and religious organizations will be compelled to sexually integrate in positions of priesthood, ministry, and other positions, with a ratio of men to women. This will be done under the supervision and control of government bureaucrats and federal courts.

As in other areas of life, religious beliefs and organized churches will have to be practiced in accordance with standards determined by government boards, government commissions, and other government agencies, with enforcement by the federal courts if necessary.

As in other areas of life under the control of the ERA, sexually balanced integration in religious organizations and offices must take priority over the private wishes and beliefs of private members and officers in positions of churches and religious organizations.

The fact that the church believes that a woman should not be admitted to priesthood or to the ministry will become secondary and subordinated to computerized sexually balanced integration pursuant to the ERA if it becomes law.

Thus, under the ERA, federal courts will order that a certain quota of women be admitted to the priesthood or ministry and to other offices in churches and religious organizations.

Therefore, while the ERA may not be able to take away your

personal beliefs and convictions in religion, the courts can and will keep you from practicing those beliefs and convictions, if they are to be inconsistent with sexually balanced integration pursuant to the ERA.

What will happen to the freedom to worship in religion if the ERA becomes law?

In many ways the ERA will, if adopted, deal death blows to freedom of choice in living, stifle and paralyze personal incentive, and place chains on one's right to beliefs, to actions, and on one's right to live peacefully.

With the passage of the ERA, private life will become puppet to government power. Socialism coupled to totalitarianism will, at the sacrifice of democracy, have attained an unparalled height in our society.

The privacy of the American citizen will be dealt a devastating blow with passage of the ERA.

Freedom now enjoyed in the relations between man and woman, husband and wife, and parent and child will be taken away, to a large extent, by passage of the ERA. Agitation by the Movement and imposition of the ERA on such relations will greatly cripple and in many cases destroy freedom.

Of course such sorry conditions will certainly be detrimental to children's normal and happy development.

The philosophy and actions of the Movement, along with the threats and legal battles brought about by the ERA, will no doubt disrupt freedom in marriages, in parent and child relations, and in the whole family, as well as in other human relations. Such philosophy and actions will destroy the present structure of society.

Win or lose? Which will it be for man, woman, child, and society if the ERA becomes law?